Militant

MICHAEL CRICK

Militant

faber and faber

LONDON·BOSTON

First published in 1984
by Faber and Faber Limited
3 Queen Square London WC1N 3AU
Printed in Great Britain by
Redwood Burn Limited
Trowbridge Wiltshire
All rights reserved

© Michael Crick, 1984

British Library Cataloguing in Publication Data

Crick, Michael
Militant
1. Labour Party—Great Britain   2. Communism
—Great Britain—History—20th century
I. Title
324.24107   JN1129.L3

ISBN 0–571–13256–1

Contents

CONTENTS

Preface and Acknowledgements

Seven hundred Labour Party members, most of them young, had assembled one evening in the main hall of the Friends' Meeting House opposite Euston Station in London. It was just one of a series of rallies organized by the Militant tendency around the country in the period immediately following Mrs Thatcher's resounding victory at the polls in June 1983. But the atmosphere of the meeting was quite unlike any of the other Labour gatherings in the post-election period. It was euphoric, not depressed, more of a celebration than a post-mortem.

It is likely that the date, 9 June 1983, will haunt many Labour Party activists for years to come. That day saw the worst Labour vote per candidate in any general election since the party was established in 1900. In every previous poll in the post-war period Labour had won between 11 million and 14 million votes. This time, however, fewer than $8\frac{1}{2}$ million people had supported Labour. True, the party had won 209 seats, but only thanks to the fact that Labour support was concentrated in the industrial areas of Britain, in Scotland, Wales and the North.

Throughout the hot summer of 1983 the Labour Party was in a depressed mood. Spirits were not lifted by the fact that now, almost as soon as one election was over, Labour activists were having to go through another—this time to choose a new leader and deputy leader. After the long evenings trudging from doorstep to doorstep and weekends writing out addresses on envelopes, most party workers wanted a break from active politics, a chance to reflect on what had gone wrong. It was a time for staying at home with the family, spending evenings out in the garden and enjoying the particularly fine weather.

But the young Militant supporters in the Friends' Meeting House that warm June evening did not feel like that. They had something to shout about. On the platform sat two of Militant's well-known senior figures: Peter Taaffe from Birkenhead, who had edited *Militant* ever since it started, and the South African, Ted Grant, *Militant*'s political editor and spiritual leader. Beside them, though, were two more recent stars, the cause of that evening's self-congratulation: Terry Fields from Liverpool and David Nellist from Coventry, who had just become the first two members of Militant to be elected to the House of Commons.

The audience heard not of the millions of people who had deserted Labour but of the 63,000 votes for the five Militant candidates. One speaker proclaimed: 'Our army is on the march ... we've now got two MPs into Parliament.' He added that these Marxists in the Commons were just the first of a 'team' of many more to follow. A comparison was even made between their success and the election of Keir Hardie as one of the first two Labour MPs in 1900. The audience was told that Labour's campaign had been waged well only on the streets of Brighton Kemptown, Liverpool Broadgreen, Bradford North, Coventry South-East and the Isle of Wight. In these places, apparently, Labour had fought the election on 'socialist ideas': the message was that the party could easily have returned to office had it stood on Militant policies in every seat. Apart from the five Militant supporters who had contested seats in the election, not once was any other Labour candidate spoken of favourably. At no point

10

during the two-hour meeting did any speaker refer to the election for a new Labour Party leader. Any foreigners sitting in the hall that night might have thought they were witnessing the celebrations of a party which had just recorded its first successes in a parliamentary election. They would have been right.

This book is the story of that party, probably Trotsky's most successful group of followers in Britain, known internally as the Revolutionary Socialist League, publicly called the Militant tendency.* Militant is more than just a well organized and successful far-left Labour Party pressure group: its programme, aims and policies are not just a more extreme version of the views of Tony Benn or Eric Heffer. Its philosophy descends directly from Marx, Engels, Lenin and Trotsky, and virtually nobody else. As a result the tendency believes in the kinds of methods, policies and goals which would be rejected totally by most ordinary Labour Party members. Because it is a revolutionary group, membership involves far more than just licking envelopes, arranging public meetings and sending out newsletters. To be a member of Militant is almost to adopt a new way of life, which consumes most of one's spare time, energy and cash. Many who eventually leave the tendency are burned out and never again become involved in politics. In some ways

---

* The political organization associated with the newspaper *Militant* was originally called the Revolutionary Socialist League (RSL). Indeed, the RSL preceded *Militant* itself by eight years. The editors of *Militant* have always publicly denied the existence of the RSL, and nowadays the name has largely fallen into disuse inside the organization. Many journalists refer to the organization as 'Militant Tendency' (with a capital 'T' and often without the definite article). This is wrong. Although Militant does refer to itself, internally and externally, as 'the tendency', or 'our tendency', this term is used only in the same way that internally it occasionally calls itself a 'group' or an 'organization'. The word 'tendency' is never given a capital 'T'. Throughout the book I will refer to the organization simply as Militant, or as the Militant tendency (without a capital 'T') or, in the early stages, as the Revolutionary Socialist League. I shall use *Militant*, in italics, when referring to the tendency's newspaper.

Militant has more in common with religion than with democratic politics.

The Labour Party battle over Militant has received a great deal of coverage in the press, on radio and on television, and media treatment has itself played an important part in the drama. But in spite of this extensive publicity very few members of the public understand who or what the Militant tendency is. Militant with a capital 'M' is often confused with militants with a small 'm'. Some people still think the term 'Militant tendency' refers to the whole of the Labour far left and includes people such as Tony Benn. This false picture is often created, even encouraged, by certain parts of the press. For a long time it was widely believed in some circles that the left-wing Labour candidate in the famous Bermondsey by-election, Peter Tatchell, was associated with Militant; it is difficult to say who was more embarrassed by this, Militant or Tatchell. His strong support for gay rights and other issues popular with middle-class Labour activists indicates that Tatchell could not possibly be a member of Militant.

I first encountered Militant when I helped to set up a Labour Party Young Socialists branch in Stockport in 1974. It was only weeks before Militant took the branch over, and I watched with a mixture of annoyance and admiration as Militant carried out its operation. I realized then that Militant was more than just a newspaper, but I was not quite sure what. Frustrated by my work in the Young Socialists, I decided thereafter to concentrate on the Labour Party itself.

I did not really encounter Militant again until I became a journalist with ITN in January 1980, at a time when the Labour Party National Executive was being urged to take action against the tendency. It struck me then that Militant was a good story waiting to be told, and as the Militant saga continued over the next three years I became increasingly surprised that no journalist had ever made a serious attempt to tell it. Eventually I came to the conclusion that I would have to do the job myself.

So what is the Militant tendency? How exactly is Militant organized? Where does it get its funds? What precisely does it stand for? What is its ultimate goal? Why has it had so much success? To what extent has that success been exaggerated? How will Militant do in the future? This book aims to deal with these questions, but it is also a book about the Labour Party itself, revealing much about how the party works at all levels and detailing the events that led to the leadership's eventual decision to take disciplinary action against Militant. The book is not meant to be a hatchet job on Militant. Certainly it contains things the tendency will not like to see in print, but Militant's leaders will admit, I hope, if only to themselves, that it is a fair account.

The work is based partly on *Militant*, the tendency's newspaper, its other official publications and a large number of secret internal documents which have leaked out of the organization. The most important source, however, has been a series of discussions and interviews with more than seventy people, nearly all of them Labour Party members. These have included Militant members, Labour Party officials, MPs, trade union officers and journalists. Particularly helpful have been more than fifteen Militant defectors, former members of the tendency who have been prepared to talk about the organization and their life in it.

Militant's leaders have given me only limited assistance. They did arrange interviews for me for the very first chapter I wrote, 'Militant Merseyside'. Afterwards it was made clear that further help would depend on the Militant leadership's seeing that chapter. With some reluctance I showed it to them. Since then, they have always been 'too busy' to meet me. However, perhaps I ought to thank *Militant* editor Peter Taaffe, if only for saving me considerable time and effort.

Many of the people I interviewed and who helped me wish

to remain anonymous, for obvious reasons. I am grateful for the time they were able to spare me. Those whom I can thank publicly are, in alphabetical order: Mike Barnes, Barrie Clarke, Ian Craig, Ken Cure, Jimmy Deane, Pete Duncan, Pat Edlin, Keith Ellis, Frank Field, Rob Gibson, Alistair Graham, Terry Harrison, Richard Hart, Millie Haston, Ellis Hillman, Sean Hughes, Charles James, Gavin Kennedy, Tony Lane, Sinna Mani, David Mason, Terry McDonald, Tony Page, Greg Pope, Allan Roberts, Eddie Roderick, Nigel Stanley, Russell Tuck, Lord Underhill, Mitchell Upfold, Neil Vann, Richard Venton, Mark Walker, Frank Ward, Alex and Frances Wood, and Margaret Young.

For their assistance I must also thank the staff in the cuttings libraries at ITN and the *Liverpool Post and Echo*; Stephen Bird, the archivist at Walworth Road; and the staff of the libraries at the universities of Oxford, Hull and Sussex, at the London School of Economics and Manchester Polytechnic, and at the British Newspaper Library at Colindale. My thanks also go to those who kindly read all or part of my manuscript and commented on it: my father, John Crick, and mother, Patricia Crick; my ITN colleagues, Jackie Ashley, Andrew Curry, Elinor Goodman, Lawrence McGinty, Paul McKee and David Walter; Simon Jenkins of *The Economist*; Michael Patchett-Joyce, Rosaleen Hughes, Jeremy Mayhew and Bill Hamilton of A. M. Heath; Tim Pearce, who did a lot of the detailed and painstaking research. Finally, I am particularly grateful to Andrew Franklin, who encouraged the idea, and Sarah Hardie, who saw it through.

M. C.
December 1983

1

'I Call This an Outrage'

When the Labour Party National Executive Committee (NEC) decided, in February 1983, to expel five members of the Editorial Board of *Militant*, it was not the first time the Labour Party had tried to take action against a Marxist newspaper within its ranks. There was an important precedent and one which must have been disturbingly familiar to the then party leader, Michael Foot.

Nearly thirty years before, in the spring of 1954, the NEC had decided that 'Persons associated in any way with the editing and sale [of a journal called *Socialist Outlook*], or contributing to that journal, are declared to be ineligible for membership of the Labour Party.' The NEC minutes stated: 'From complaints that have been received it seems evident that a Trotskyist organization is functioning within the Labour Party.'[1]

That decision in 1954 prompted a ferocious attack in *Tribune*, the leading journal of the Labour left. Under the heading 'I Call This an Outrage', a former editor of *Tribune* wrote:

For the first time in its history, so far as I am aware, the leaders of the Labour Party have taken steps to suppress a newspaper.

15

The article went on:

> Such a decree might fittingly be issued within a Fascist or
> Communist Party. That it should be issued by the leaders
> of a democratic party is an outrage.
>
> The good name of the Labour Party requires that this
> stupid, cowardly and totalitarian edict should be rescinded
> at the coming Labour Party Conference and that the
> National Executive should be instructed not to tamper
> further with the elementary principles of freedom.[2]

The author of the article was Michael Foot. In 1982 *Tribune*
was to reprint his words more than once, in a new campaign
against the Labour Party NEC.[3] This time *Militant* was the
Trotskyist paper the Executive was trying to suppress, and
Michael Foot was leading the action.

Ever since the Labour Party established itself as the
unchallenged representative of the British working class, the
party leadership has constantly been in conflict with groups
on the left who have felt that the party has not been sufficiently radical in its methods and policies. These groups
range from revolutionary Marxists to what is often termed
the 'legitimate left' (by those further to the right). They
include groups, initially outside, who have decided deliberately to join the Labour Party in order to influence it from
within, as well as groups of like-minded party members who
have come together to press for some cause or other. But no
matter how strong their dissent, and no matter how limited
their prospects of advancement, these factions have usually
preferred to remain inside the party—aware no doubt that
groups which have left the party have always suffered drasti-
cally. The result has been a long history of disciplinary action
by the party establishment against left-wing pressure groups
and 'newspapers'. And one of the great ironies of this history
has been that often the rebels of one generation have become
the establishment of the next.

The history of Labour Party internal discipline did not really begin until the 1920s. In 1918 the party had introduced individual membership: until then it had been simply a federation of affiliated bodies, such as trade unions and socialist societies. One of the affiliated societies was a Marxist group, the Social Democratic Federation; another was the British Socialist Party, which later became the British Communist Party. Until 1918 all party members had to belong to an affiliated organization rather than directly to the party. The advent of individual membership was to bring with it the problem of what to do when individual members grouped together in non-affiliated organizations outside the party's control. The same year, 1918, saw the Labour Party commit itself fully to socialism: the new constitution contained the famous Clause IV, which calls for common ownership. But while the party appeared to move leftwards, many felt that for electoral reasons, and in the wake of the Russian Revolution, Labour would have to distance itself from the ideas of Bolshevism if it was to become a serious party of government.

When the British Communist Party (CP) was formally established in 1920, it applied almost immediately for affiliation to the Labour Party. The Communist leaders pointed to the example of the left-wing Independent Labour Party which had been affiliated to the Labour Party since 1900; they argued that they should be allowed to join in the same way. But time and again in the early 1920s Labour conferences turned down the Communists' requests. The leadership argued that the CP's aims were not in accord with Labour's 'constitution, principles and programme' and said that the Communists would be loyal to the Soviet-led Communist International (Comintern) rather than to the Labour Party. Labour was perhaps right to be cautious: Lenin had urged his British comrades to support the Labour Party Secretary Arthur Henderson 'as a rope supports the hanged'.[4]

It took some years for Labour to expel those Communists already inside its ranks. Under the existing rules Communists were for several years allowed to speak at Conference and even to serve as Labour councillors and MPs: one case was Sharurji Saklatvala (the last coloured MP in Britain), who in 1922 was elected for Labour in Battersea North while openly being a Communist as well. Gradually, though, the loopholes were closed: Communists were barred from being individual Labour Party members and from selection as Labour candidates, and affiliated unions were asked not to choose Communists as delegates to the Labour Conference. And in 1927 the NEC disbanded ten local Labour parties, most of them in London, because they had effectively been taken over by the CP.

Between 1928 and 1935 the problem of Communists in the party died down; the Comintern was now advising its supporters not to link up with the 'social fascists' in Western social democratic parties. After the 1935 election, though, the Communist General Secretary, Harry Pollitt, once again applied for affiliation for his party. At one point it looked as though the Labour Conference might agree, but a series of show trials staged by Stalin in the Soviet Union ruined the British Communists' chances. They did not give up, however. A new tactic was employed instead. Over the next four years CP members secretly infiltrated hundreds of local Labour parties. Douglas Hyde, once news editor of of the Communist *Daily Worker*, later revealed that he himself had organized a gradual Communist takeover of his local Labour Party in Surrey, secretly signing up the most promising members one by one. Eventually when Hyde had recruited a large number of individuals to the CP, he gathered them together for what they all thought was just a meeting of local left-wing Labour Party members.

18

When all had arrived I revealed that everyone present was already a Communist Party member, and suddenly they realized what had happened and just what strength the Party already had in the local Labour movement. Then we got down to business.... From then on we functioned as a Communist Party group, continuing to keep our membership secret and working inside the Labour Party and Trades Council.[5]

After Munich, though, the CP decided that under-cover members should leave as a political demonstration against the Labour leadership. 'Almost the whole of our group resigned from the Labour Party, getting maximum publicity for their action.... the Labour Party in that Division was all but wrecked, losing all its active and leading members at one move.'[6]

Another 'entrist' at this time was the young Denis Healey, chairman of the Oxford University Labour Club while openly carrying a CP card as well. 'I read all the basic books, but I never believed in it,' Healey said years later. 'It was more a reaction to Nazism. The really big issue was the rise of Hitler and the coming war. Any young man who was interested in stopping the war became a Communist at Oxford, whether he joined the Party or not.'[7]

Towards the end of the 1930s disciplinary action was being taken not only against Communists but also against members who were working politically with the CP. Many socialists believed that the most important political priority at that time was to construct a United or Popular Front against fascism, involving socialists, Communists and even Liberals and Conservatives.

These were the years of Victor Gollancz's Left Book Club, the start of the newspaper *Tribune* and the sending of the International Brigade to fight against Franco in Spain. Thousands of socialists worked side by side with members of the CP: this did not necessarily mean that they were Communists themselves or that they were subject to every whim of Stalin's Communist International, much though some Labour Party officials may have believed that. True, the idea of 'Popular Fronts' with other parties had originated with the Communist International, but these socialists were not simply being manipulated by the CP. There was a genuine desire for unity against fascism; advocates of the 'Popular Front' were not necessarily Communist infiltrators.

At first the left-wing Socialist League, affiliated to the party, was the main proponent of 'unity' in the fight against fascism. The leaders of the League were Sir Stafford Cripps, the MP and wealthy barrister who provided most of the money; Aneurin Bevan and George Strauss, also MPs; Harold Laski; and G. D. H. Cole. Less well-known League leaders were two young journalists from *Tribune*: Michael Foot and Barbara Betts (the young Barbara Castle). Because it advocated 'unity' the League was disaffiliated in 1937, and later, in January 1939, Cripps was expelled; a few months later four others followed, including Bevan and Strauss. It did not take long for the rebels to be rehabilitated, however. By 1942 Cripps was a Labour member of Churchill's Cabinet, and he later went on to be Chancellor of the Exchequer under Attlee. Bevan helped to draft the 1945 manifesto and served with distinction in the post-war Labour Cabinet. Strauss was to be a junior Minister under Attlee and eventually Father of the House of Commons.

Members of the Labour Party youth section were also regarded as a 'nuisance' by the Labour leadership before the war. The majority left-wing group in the Labour League of Youth was led by Ted Willis, later to achieve fame as a writer. On the opposing side of the League was the young George Brown. The Willis faction of the Labour League of Youth Advisory Committee (its Executive Committee) decided to ignore the League's official paper, *New Nation*, because it was produced by Transport House. Instead they published their own journal, *Advance!*, which at one point achieved a remarkable circulation of 50,000. Naturally they supported Cripps and Bevan in their call for a 'Popular Front'. Their reward was suspension of their committee by Transport House; after months of argument Willis and most of his comrades eventually left the Labour Party and joined the Young Communist League. After the war Willis rejoined Labour, and he has sat on the Labour benches in the House of Lords for the last twenty years.

Immediately after the war the CP hoped that its support of the wartime coalition would help its case for affiliation to the Labour Party, but its new application was rejected overwhelmingly by the 1946 Labour Conference. That year Conference also decided that no new national political organization would ever be allowed to affiliate to the party. So CP tactics changed. Rather than infiltrate the Labour Party directly, the Communists built up a whole range of 'front organizations' designed to attract and influence Labour Party members. Some of these had been established before the war and often involved 'peace' or 'friendship' with a Communist country. Among such groups were the British–Romanian Association, the British Vietnam Committee, the British–China Friendship Committee and the World Peace Council. So as not to give the game away too obviously, each group had as its chairman not a CP member but a 'fellow-traveller', someone with Communist sympathies.

The Labour Party's response to these groups was the famous (perhaps notorious) List of Proscribed Organizations, originally established in 1930 to deal with Communist infiltration then. Labour Party members were not allowed to belong to groups on the list. Among the casualties was a trade union official, Jim Mortimer, who was forced to leave the party in the early 1950s for being a member of the British–China Friendship Association. Thirty years later, as Labour

Party General Secretary, Mortimer was to establish another kind of list, a 'List of Approved Organizations', in his fight against Militant.

Nearly all groups on the Proscribed List were CP bodies, but in 1951 the name of the Socialist Fellowship was added. This was a left-wing pressure group designed to bring together MPs, trade unionists and rank-and-file party members. It had several branches around the country, held national conferences and had its own policy. But in time the Socialist Fellowship increasingly came to be dominated by a secret Trotskyist organization called The Club, which was run by Gerry Healy, a former member of the Trotskyist Revolutionary Communist Party and today leader of the Workers' Revolutionary Party. Closely associated with the Socialist Fellowship was the newspaper *Socialist Outlook*, which in 1954[8] was also banned on the grounds that some of its contributors were 'known for their previous association with the Trotskyist Revolutionary Communist Party'.[9] The NEC's action led to the *Tribune* article by Michael Foot quoted above.

At the time Foot and the group around Aneurin Bevan—the Bevanites—worked closely with Gerry Healy and his newspaper. Indeed, when *Socialist Outlook* was eventually forced to fold because of a libel action, Gerry Healy began writing for *Tribune*. (Years later Michael Foot was to be reminded by Eric Heffer of his close associations with Healy, much to Foot's embarrassment.) The Bevanites argued that the banning of *Socialist Outlook* was just the first step in a large-scale witch-hunt against the Labour left. Foot told a meeting in London that if the NEC got away with banning *Socialist Outlook*, it would 'look around for the next one on the list'.[10] It was exactly the same argument as that used by the left today against the banning of *Militant*. In the 1950s the left's fears were understandable. The period saw several moves against Aneurin Bevan and his supporters, Foot included.

22

The left–right conflict intensified in 1951 with Bevan's famous resignation from the dying Attlee Government (along with Harold Wilson and John Freeman). There had been left-wing discontent before, but Bevan now provided the left with a leader outside the Government around whom to rally, and the split persisted when Labour went into Opposition. In this period the party outside Parliament—in the form of the Conference and the NEC—was virtually run by the big three union leaders, Arthur Deakin of the Transport and General Workers' Union, Tom Williamson of the General and Municipal Workers and Will Lawther, the miners' leader, who achieved particular notoriety at the Morecambe Conference in 1952, when he shouted 'Shut yer gob!' to constituency delegates who interrupted one of his speeches.[11] Between them the three bosses controlled nearly half the union Conference votes, and union votes altogether effectively elected eighteen places on the twenty-eight strong NEC. Meanwhile the constituencies, who elected seven NEC members, were swinging to the left, and at Morecambe in 1952 six of their places were filled with Bevanites, with Herbert Morrison and Hugh Dalton losing their places. Over the next few years the union bosses, aided by Morrison, Dalton and Hugh Gaitskell in Parliament, were to battle it out with the Bevanites.

The accusations against the Bevanites will be familiar to observers of the modern Labour Party. Attlee spoke of them as 'a party within a party, with separate leadership, separate meetings, supported by its own press'.[12] In Parliament the Bevanite group of MPs was forced to open up its meetings to outsiders and in the end had to disband altogether. Quite apart from the action against *Socialist Outlook*, it was suggested by some on the right that *Tribune* should be outlawed as well.

Accounts of party meetings from the period show they were just as bitter, if not worse, than those of today. Richard Crossman said that the NEC had a 'detestable atmosphere';

23

according to Ian Mikardo, Tom Driberg was 'wrung out like a dish rag' after each meeting, 'desperate for a large drink'; Michael Foot described Parliamentary Labour Party (PLP) meetings as 'gruesome'.[13] Yet in the 1950s the policy differences between the two sides were minor compared with those of the modern Labour Party.

The feud reached its peak in the spring of 1955, as Bevan and Gaitskell squared up for the contest to succeed Attlee. In March Bevan attacked Attlee in a Commons debate on nuclear weapons and was promptly expelled from the PLP. Soon it looked almost certain that Bevan would also be expelled from the Labour Party itself—for the second time. Hugh Gaitskell and Arthur Deakin saw it as their chance finally to get rid of him. As the crucial NEC meeting approached, Bevan looked doomed. Deakin seemed to have sewn up most of the trade union and women members—the majority of the NEC. The episode had remarkable parallels with recent events. As with the expulsion of the Militant leaders in 1983, the turmoil erupted when a general election was likely at any moment (polling day was two months later), but many right-wingers, far from being reluctant to take action because of the prospect of going to the polls, believed that Bevan was an electoral liability and that his expulsion would increase the party's chances of victory. In the end, however, against the odds and almost by accident, Bevan survived by one vote.

Within two years Bevan was *de facto* second in command of the party.[14] In the poll for the new Shadow Cabinet immediately after the 1955 election, the PLP voted Bevan into seventh position—just three months after having voted to eject him from their ranks. In the autumn of 1957, when the two former arch-enemies, Gaitskell and Bevan, had become leader of the party and Shadow Foreign Secretary respectively, they gave the press a unique political photo. Just before the Brighton Conference the two men could be seen walking

24

arm in arm along the sea front at Brighton. 'Remarkable,' said journalist Leslie Hunter to a nearby trade unionist. 'Remarkable?' came the quick reply. 'That's not remarkable, it's a bloody miracle.'[15] And by 1959 Bevan was deputy leader.

Michael Foot, perhaps because he was less important, was luckier than Bevan and always managed to hold on to his party card. But he was less fortunate in the PLP. After Bevan's death in 1960 Foot returned to the Commons as MP for his hero's old seat, Ebbw Vale. But not long after, the future Labour leader was one of five left-wing MPs who lost the whip for voting against the Conservative defence esti-mates (the instructions were to abstain). Considering the widespread dissent within the PLP in modern times, it seems surprising that such extreme action should have been taken, but that was how the party worked under the leadership of Hugh Gaitskell. PLP membership was not restored to Foot and his colleagues until after Harold Wilson's election in 1963, which meant that Foot could not vote in the leadership poll. During his long career in Parliament Foot achieved the distinction of being perhaps the greatest rebel of them all: in the period from 1945 to 1970, when he joined the front bench, Foot probably voted against his party more than any other Labour MP; on the Tory side only Enoch Powell rebelled more often.[16]

This chapter has tried to put the events of the recent Militant story into historical perspective. The Labour Party has a long history of expulsions, of discipline by the leadership against left-wing rebel groups that have been considered electorally damaging or just politically irritating: Militant is only the most recent. What is so fascinating about the party's history is that rebels should so easily become leaders. As far as this story is concerned, it is particularly ironic that three of the main leaders of the recent campaign against Militant should themselves have all incurred the wrath of party officials at one time or another: Denis Healey, the Communist 'infiltrator' in the 1930s; Jim Mortimer, member of a proscribed organization; and, above all, Michael Foot.

But perhaps more important, so far as the story of Militant is concerned, is that the memories of heavy-handed discipline in the 1930s and 1950s were to have a profound effect on the party in later years. Harold Wilson's Labour Party was to be much more tolerant than Hugh Gaitskell's; expulsions were rare, and the Proscribed List fell into disuse simply because nobody bothered to update it. Ron Hayward claims that when he became General Secretary in 1972 he personally burned the Transport House files on left-wingers. By the 1970s the NEC contained many people who had once experienced party discipline themselves. They were determined not to allow a return to what they saw as the 'McCarthyism' of the past.

2

The Permanent Revolutionary

From the late 1920s to the present day the history of British Trotskyism has been a tale of splits and mergers, of internal wrangling and bitterness, of argument rather than action. Each of the successive sects and factions seems to have detested its Trotskyist rivals far more than any of its natural enemies on the right of British politics. Uninitiated outsiders have considerable difficulty in working out the subtle political differences between the various groupings. The key point to grasp in studying the revolutionary left of British politics is that questions of tactics are often more divisive than ideology, personalities a more frequent cause of strife than policy. The followers of Leon Trotsky, like those of Jesus Christ, may all believe in the teachings of the same man, but they have rarely been united.

Trotsky's followers have suffered possibly more divisions in Britain than anywhere else. And what makes the progression particularly difficult to understand is that as one sect has replaced another, each has felt obliged to compose its name from a holy list of about twelve words, among them: Workers, Labour, Socialist, International, Revolutionary, Marxist, Communist, Militant, Group, Party, Tendency and League. According to the rules of the game of 'Select-a-Sect', you can pick any two or three from the above list and make yourself a new Trotskyist grouping. You might end up with the Workers' International League, the Militant Labour League, the International Marxist Group, the Revolutionary Socialist League, the Revolutionary Communist Party or the Workers' Revolutionary Party. All of these, and dozens more, exist now or have existed at one time or another.

After Stalin succeeded to the leadership of the Soviet Communist Party on Lenin's death in 1924, his opponents within the Soviet Union began to gather around Lenin's right-hand man during the Russian Revolution and founder of the Red Army, Leon Trotsky. They adopted the title of the Left Opposition. Apart from personality differences, the division between the two men was over which course the revolution should follow from that point onwards. Since 1906 Trotsky had believed in the idea of permanent revolution and was convinced that his country could achieve socialism only if there were worldwide revolution. In Trotsky's view, it had been possible for the Bolsheviks to achieve power purely within national boundaries, but it would be impossible for the Soviet Union to proceed to socialism without revolutionary developments elsewhere. Stalin, on the other hand, proposed 'socialism in one country', partly in opposition to Trotsky's position. The Soviet leader believed that his country could create a socialist society on its own.

The division between the two men spread to the Communist International (the Comintern or Third International), the organization founded in Moscow in 1919 to unite those parties formerly in the Second International that supported the Bolshevik Revolution. (The Second International had split in 1914 over the member parties' different attitudes to the First World War, and afterwards the 'reformist' members formed their own Socialist International.) In the Comintern Trotsky's supporters adopted the title of the International Left Opposition (ILO). Eventually the differences between Stalin and Trotsky became so great, however, that in 1929 Trotsky was banished to Turkey, and his supporters were purged from the Communist International, which had become totally dominated by Stalin. But the Trotskyists kept up their struggle.

In Britain Trotsky gained no significant support until the early 1930s, and then it was split into two groups. One group worked within the British Communist Party until it was expelled in 1932; the other operated inside the Independent Labour Party (ILP), which until 1932 was affiliated to the Labour Party. From the very beginning Trotskyists in this country were divided over how they should proceed. Such tactical differences have afflicted British Trotskyism to this day.

Long after his expulsion from the Soviet Union, Trotsky himself remained convinced that his followers should be loyal to the Communist International, even though they were actually banned from it, and that they should work within Communist parties. According to his biographer, Isaac Deutscher, Trotsky was initially totally opposed to the idea that his supporters should form their own Fourth International to challenge the Comintern:

> Trotsky believed that with all their flaws and vices the Communist parties still represented the militant vanguard of the working classes. The Opposition's place was with that vanguard. If he and his followers were to turn their backs on it, they would voluntarily go out into the wilderness into which Stalin was driving them.[1]

But from 1933 Trotsky's position changed. The failure of the German Communists (the KPD) to unite with the German Social Democrats against Nazism had finally convinced him that no further progress could be made inside Communist parties. From now on he was to recommend his famous policy of 'entrism' (sometimes spelt 'entryism'—strong advocates are said to have 'enteritis') to supporters in all Western countries: they should abandon

Communist parties and instead 'enter' the mass social democratic parties. The most notable example of entrism by Trotskyists occurred in France, where Trotsky had a strong following. There he advised them to join the French socialist party, the SFIO, and to 'carry their revolutionary programme to the masses'. This radical change of tactics became known as the 'French turn', and Trotsky recommended the same entrist policy to his supporters in other countries: the United States, Chile, Belgium and Spain. In Britain he had advocated entrism as early as 1933 but did not, as might have been expected, recommend 'entering' the main mass party, the Labour Party. Since his British supporters were numerically very weak, Trotsky felt they would have more influence inside the smaller ILP.

In 1932 the ILP had disaffiliated from the Labour Party in an argument over whether ILP MPs should be answerable to the Labour Party or to the ILP. Over the next few years the ILP started moving leftwards but also lost most of its members. Trotsky was confident, though, that at some future date a more left-wing ILP would come to reaffiliate to the Labour Party. He saw the potential situation in Britain as a series of levers. His followers could have a significant effect as a lever within the ILP;[2] in turn, he hoped, an ILP under their influence, once reaffiliated, would act as a radical lever inside the Labour Party itself.

But again Trotsky's British troops were divided: not all thought the ILP worth entering. Many favoured a more direct approach and entered the Labour Party instead. By 1936 Trotsky accepted that ILP entry should be abandoned: although Trotskyist numbers had increased sixfold, within the ILP there had been no political victories. Entrism within the Labour Party, it was now thought, might be politically more profitable. Trotsky wrote to his British supporters:

It is understood that, regardless of how we enter, we will

have a secret faction from the very beginning. Our subsequent actions will depend on our progress within the LP [Labour Party]. It is very important that we do not lay ourselves open at the beginning to attacks from the LP bureaucracy, which will result in our expulsion without having gained any appreciable strength.... While it is necessary for the revolutionary party to maintain its independence at all times, a revolutionary group of a few hundred comrades is not a revolutionary party and can work most effectively at present by opposition to the social patriots within the mass parties.[3]

Independent existence for the Trotskyists at that time just would not work—the numbers were too small. Nevertheless, it is clear from Trotsky's writings that he saw entrism as very much a short-term tactic.

Modern Trotskyists are still divided over the purpose of entrism. Two types of entrism have evolved, both of which cite Trosky's work as justification. One is the 'raiding party' type of entrism: Trotskyists go into a mass party to win converts and then leave as a much strengthened force. The work in the ILP in the 1930s had turned out to be of this type, and, as we have seen in chapter 1, Lenin argued for a similar tactic in the Labour Party in the 1920s. The other sort of entrism, termed 'Waiting for Lefty' by Tariq Ali,[4] involves joining a party at a time of social and political upheaval in order to be in the forefront of the revolution when the right moment comes. The long-term secret entrism later adopted by Militant—sometimes called 'deep entrism'—seems to be a modified version of this.

In the mid-1930s in Britain one set of Trotskyists—called the Balham Group—operated within the Labour Party in south London and were active within the Socialist League. The party authorities knew what these Trotskyists were up to but did not pay them too much attention, since

31

the NEC was concerned at that time about a much bigger problem: infiltration by members of the Communist Party.

Another Trotskyist group (internally known as the Revolutionary Socialist League) became active in the Labour Party youth section, the Labour League of Youth, rallying around a monthly paper called *Young Militant*. By 1937 this group was selling nearly 2,000 copies of its journal and was the biggest Trotskyist group yet seen in Britain. That year it publicly adopted the title of the Militant Labour League and later its paper was simply called *Militant*. Here was a 'Militant tendency' active in the Labour Party nearly twenty years before the present Militant tendency was even set up. This group, like its successor, quickly learned that young members of the Labour Party are a good source of recruits.

The Militant Labour League was not the first to use the name 'Militant': it had been borrowed from Trotsky's followers in America, who had been publishing a newspaper called *The Militant* since 1928. Several thousand copies of the paper had crossed the Atlantic to be sold here. But the name 'Militant' is not the only link with the present-day group. It is at this point in the story that we first meet the man who has been one of the leading figures of British Trotskyism for nearly half a century and who today is the spiritual leader of the Militant tendency: Ted Grant.

In the mid-1930s a group of six South African Trotskyists arrived in ones and twos from Johannesburg. All had been involved in left-wing politics in their homeland, organizing strikes among black workers and suffering police harassment and arrests. But the prospects at home were extremely limited: even left-wing whites in South Africa did not trust them. Britain was a more likely starting-point for the revolution than South Africa and was obviously the place to go. Grant was the first to take the boat trip from Johannesburg to London, probably in 1935 or 1936 but possibly as early as 1934.[5] (Ted Grant is not his real name. He adopted the name

32

for security reasons when he arrived in Britain.) Another to make the journey from Johannesburg was Millie Lee (later Millie Haston). Today, retired and living in Clapham, she reviews Ted Grant's subsequent career with astonishment:

> Ted had always been a full-time revolutionary, right from the age of 17 when we first met him, but he was never an organizer. Ted never seemed to have the sort of personality which would attract his own following, but nevertheless he did. And he's saying exactly the same things now as he was saying then—like a gramophone record that got stuck forty years ago.[6]

Within a year of joining the Militant Labour League the six South Africans had broken away to form their own group, the Workers' International League (WIL). It occurred not so much because of political disagreements but as a result of personality clashes and resentment towards the South African newcomers. Others to leave with them were a Scotsman, Jock Haston, and Gerry Healy, who had left the Communist Party and recently joined the Militant Labour League after buying a copy of *Young Militant*, at a rally in Hyde Park.

In September 1938 Trotsky and his followers from around the world held a conference at a house in Périgny, a village just outside Paris, called the 'Lausanne Conference' for security reasons. Present were twenty delegates from eleven countries. This was the founding conference of the Fourth International, a worldwide organization of Trotskyists who saw it as the natural successor to the Second and Third (Communist) Internationals, which they now regarded as 'morally dead'. The British delegation to the conference came from the Militant Labour League, not the breakaway Workers' International League. Afterwards the Militant Labour League became the Fourth International's official British section. The Labour Party responded by proscribing it.

So during the key event in Trotskyist history Ted Grant and his comrades were left out in the cold. Furthermore, their Workers' International League was tiny—just nineteen members to start with—compared with the rival Militant Labour League, whose membership numbered several hundred. Grant's group was ignored by Trotsky and the Fourth International. Because of this disagreement Ted Grant never met the 'Old Man' in the period between Grant's arrival from South Africa and Trotsky's assassination in 1940.

Soon the Militant Labour League publicly adopted its internal title, the Revolutionary Socialist League (RSL). Meanwhile Grant and the small WIL set out on their own road, determined to wrest from the RSL the honour of being the Fourth International's British section. They started a new monthly journal, *Youth for Socialism* (later called *Socialist Appeal*), which Grant edited, and a newspaper, *Workers' International News*. Even though there was a war on, the WIL was very active and held regular public meetings. It is interesting to note that at one meeting in August 1941, on the anniversary of Trotsky's assassination, the two main speakers were Ted Grant and Gerry Healy. The chairman that evening was Syd Bidwell, who today is Labour MP for Ealing Southall.

In spite of its split with the official group, the WIL carried on for a while practising entrism within the Labour Party. Ted Grant himself must have been a member of the party at this time, although it is unlikely that he was very active. Today Grant boasts of having been a Labour Party member since 1950 but omits to mention this period of membership before the war. In any case, in 1941 the WIL abandoned entrism because it saw it as a good tactic only where the reformist party was 'in a state of flux, where political life is at a high pitch and where the members are steadily moving left. It is essentially a short-term perspective for work in a milieu where favourable prospects exist for a short space of time.'[7] The wartime coalition had, in the view of the WIL, made the Labour Party a 'moribund political force'. During the war both the Labour Party and the trade unions had agreed to moderate political and industrial activities in support of the coalition. The WIL's departure from the Labour Party was a move which gave it greater scope for militant political and industrial action.

Within a few years Grant and his comrades had achieved a much stronger position than that of the rival RSL, which had remained entrist. By 1944, in fact, the RSL was so weak that the Fourth International persuaded it to merge with the WIL and to form the new Revolutionary Communist Party (RCP)—a title which greatly annoyed the official Communist Party. In effect, though, it was more of a takeover than a merger. Jock Haston became the RCP General Secretary; *Socialist Appeal* became the party's paper, with Grant continuing as editor; and the WIL took the bulk of the places on the new RCP central committee. The RCP became the Fourth International's official British section, and the first two delegates were Haston and Grant. Grant and his comrades had worked their way back into the official Trotskyist fold, and they had done so mainly through their decision to leave the temporarily 'moribund' Labour Party.

For three years British Trotskyists were almost totally united for the only time in their history. The RCP was quite successful at first, at least by its own standards: it had twelve full-time workers and perhaps as many as 600 members. It played a leading role in the increasing number of industrial disputes. At one point three RCP leaders (though not Grant) were jailed for encouraging apprentices to resist ballots for selecting 'Bevin boys' to go down the mines. Questions were asked in the Commons about the sale of *Socialist Appeal* in the coalfields, and the Cabinet even considered banning the party.[8]

In April 1944 the Home Secretary, Herbert Morrison, prepared a paper on the RCP for the War Cabinet. Grant's name was fairly prominent:

> Edward Grant. Editor of *Socialist Appeal*, aged 30, is also South African and has been connected with the Workers' International League since its inception. He was posted to the Pioneer Corps but fractured his skull before joining up and was discharged. It has proved impossible, owing to the effects of his injury, to find him alternative employment.[9]

This meant that Grant was able to carry on working full-time at politics. Indeed it seems he worked so hard that, according to the Cabinet papers, he suffered a nervous breakdown.[10]

Frank Ward was another leading member of both the WIL and then the RCP in this period. Today he works as Information Officer at the Labour Party headquarters at Walworth Road. After the war Ward was an RCP organizer in Glasgow and then Manchester, earning a meagre £2 a week. Ward remembers that Grant and Haston worked side by side as leaders of the RCP. Haston was the main organizer, as opposed to Grant, whom he remembers as a 'writer' and 'lecturer':

> He was never organized. Millie [Haston] basically edited the paper, though Ted would make the decisions. Sometimes it was impossible to get him to write the editorials; we had to lock him and Jock into a room to make them write them. On one occasion they climbed out of the window though, and nipped down to the local flea-pit.[11]

Sammy Bornstein also worked with Grant in the RCP. Today he is a Labour Party member in Finchley:

> I haven't seen him in years. But I knew him quite well. Rather colourless, never struck me as a personality. But he was able to hold an audience when he spoke. Nobody

36

really knew Ted. You'd have a drink, eye up the girls—but not Ted. He was very serious.... Ted's always been the same. Since 1945 he has been predicting a slump.[12]

As we shall see, the Ted Grant of the 1930s and 1940s was very much the same as the Ted Grant of today. People who knew him then say much the same things about him as those who work with him now. And his political outlook has hardly changed at all.

With the end of the Second World War the RCP went into decline. The wartime coalition was now over and the Labour Party was again on the political stage, making a spectacular comeback with its landslide victory in 1945. The RCP leaders, optimistic as always, predicted that Attlee would 'do a Ramsay MacDonald' and betray the labour movement. They were to be disappointed. The post-war Labour Government proceeded to nationalize the major industries and to build the welfare state. Arguments about 'betrayal' were difficult to sustain. The British economy soon moved back to full employment, and an era of growth began. The RCP's belief that capitalism was on the point of collapse started to look somewhat unconvincing. And while one Trotskyist enemy, social democracy, was succeeding in Britain, the other, Stalinism, was flourishing abroad. The Soviet Union had emerged from the war with considerable international prestige and control of Eastern Europe. The 1949 revolution in China, backed by the Soviet Union, was regarded as another feather in Stalin's cap.

Slowly the RCP broke up. The Fourth International wanted its British comrades to readopt the entrist tactic, but most of the RCP argued that the time was not right. Since the formation of the RCP in 1944, a minority group, led by Gerry Healy, had practised entrism and for several years produced a journal called *Militant*. Later Healy's group began *Socialist Outlook* for its Labour Party work (see chapter 1). The official RCP paper, Ted Grant's *Socialist Appeal*, appeared less frequently.

Gradually the minority faction had been gaining the upper hand, and for most RCP comrades entry now seemed the only option. Grant himself was not keen on the idea but did not think it worth causing internal strife over the issue. In a signed statement to a colleague he wrote:

> Discussion in the party on the question of entry has naturally provoked a crisis in the organization ... under the given conditions, the best tactic for the party is the maintenance of the independent party.
>
> The discussion has not convinced us that in the present situation entry would constitute a superior tactic. However, faced with the fact that the overwhelming majority of the leadership and the trained cadres, and a substantial section of the rank and file, are in favour of entering the Labour Party, and given that the objective situation will be a difficult one for the party, we believe that a struggle in the party [the RCP] would be sterile.[13]

So it was that when the RCP was finally disbanded in 1950 Ted Grant came to rejoin the Labour Party.

Frank Ward looks back on those years in the WIL and the RCP, the late 1930s and 1940s, as 'the age when Trotskyism grew up'. 'It was an attempt,' he says, 'to deal with what the world looked like on the limited evidence of the 1930s. Before the war it wasn't easy to see that Stalin would maintain his position in the Soviet Union, or that there would be economic expansion in the West after the war.'[14] In June 1950 the RCP General Secretary, Jock Haston, and his wife, Millie, renounced Trotskyism and joined the Labour Party. Frank Ward went with them. The rest of the RCP had no choice but to join Healy's group inside the Labour Party, The Club. But soon Healy began expelling many of the leading individuals who had joined him. The result was that three separate groups quickly formed around three key figures: Gerry Healy himself, Tony Cliff, an immigrant from Palestine, and Ted Grant. These three factions have dominated British Trotskyism to this day. (It is interesting to note that none of the three was British. All came from former parts of the British Empire: Healy from Ireland, Cliff from Palestine and Grant from South Africa.)

Healy's group, The Club, later became the Socialist Labour League and is now the Workers' Revolutionary Party (WRP). For the time being, at least, Healy kept the Fourth International franchise. Cliff's faction, the *Socialist Review* group, who were known as the 'state caps' because of their belief that the Soviet Union was state capitalist, later became the International Socialists and eventually the Socialist Workers' Party (SWP). And Grant's group went on to become the Militant tendency. Relations between the three groups have often been bitter, especially between Healy and Grant. Only four years after the parting of the ways Grant abstained at a meeting of his local Labour Party in East Islington when it voted to expel two Healyites.

In the years since the collapse of the RCP all three groups have at one time or another practised entrism inside the Labour Party. Today, though, both the SWP and the WRP reject entrism and only the Grantites have pursued the tactic consistently since 1950. Of the three, in terms of political outlook the Grant faction has changed the least from that of the old WIL and RCP.

But while the entrism of the Healy and Cliff groups eventually came up against Labour Party discipline in the 1950s and 1960s, Ted Grant and his colleagues survived this period virtually unscathed. This was largely because for a long period they were by far the least significant of the three factions. At one point in the early 1950s a Labour Party official did try to use Grant's past record to expel him from his local party in Islington, but without success. For fourteen years Grant carried on publishing insignificant Trotskyist newspapers and worked, almost unseen, within the Labour Party. Unlike Haston and Ward, but just like Healy and Cliff, Grant never gave up being a revolutionary. 'When the party disintegrated most of us found jobs and some dropped out of politics altogether,' says Frank Ward. 'But Ted had nowhere to go to. He needed a social grouping to carry on as a part-time revolutionary.'[15]

For years Grant's group was very small: probably never consisting even of fifty people at the very most. One man who stuck with Grant throughout these years was an electrical engineer from Liverpool, Jimmy Deane. Deane had worked closely with Grant since 1937, first in the WIL and then in the RCP. While Grant concerned himself with theoretical matters, Deane was a more down-to-earth politician who dealt with the practical problems: organization and industrial work. In some ways Deane had the same relationship with Grant in the barren years of the 1950s as Jock Haston had had in the 1940s. Today Deane remembers: 'After the RCP split up we kept up a whole series of publications. We did our best with the meagre resources we had. They wouldn't come out regularly—maybe every month, two months, three months. We tried to keep the light burning.'[16]

Grant stayed in London, living in a caravan at one time and then moving rapidly from one flat to another. Eventually he found work as a night telephone operator, making telephone contacts by night and political ones by day. Jimmy Deane stayed in his home town, Liverpool, and was active in the Labour Party in Walton—the only left-wing party in a city controlled by the Labour right. In 1948 Deane had helped to start a magazine in the Birkenhead Labour League of Youth called *Rally* (which stood for "Read all about the Labour League of Youth'). *Rally* survived, on and off, for a remarkably long period (often under the name *Rally for Socialism*). Sometimes the magazine was properly printed; more often it was simply duplicated. It was essentially a paper for young members of the Labour Party and campaigned vigorously for a youth charter. By 1952 *Rally* had transferred its base across the Mersey to Walton, where it was edited by Pat Wall, the Militant candidate who stood in Bradford North in 1983. Later the magazine attracted many other young socialists who were to be prominent in Militant, among them Keith Dickinson and Peter Taaffe, both members of *Militant*'s Editorial Board who were expelled in 1983.

Meanwhile in London Grant began a small magazine, *International Socialist*, which declared itself a 'rallying centre for the left in the Labour Party'. In the first issue, in February 1952, Grant declared:

> The British masses in the upheavals and convulsions of tomorrow will find the way to a Marxist policy. Armed with this, the Labour movement will overthrow capitalism and together with the workers on the Continent organize a Socialist United States of Europe. The alternatives are either Fascism and war or the victory of the working class. There can be no middle road.[17]

Buy a copy of *Militant* more than thirty years later and there on the back page, at the bottom of a list of principles for which *Militant* stands, is the same call for a 'Socialist United States of Europe'.[18] However, *International Socialist* existed for only seven issues, the last of which came out in April 1954.

Associated with the magazine was the International Socialist Group, which had actually been formed fifteen months before the first issue came out. The group had a formal organization and held regular meetings above a restaurant in the Finchley Road, in north London. Its activities, such as they were, were confined almost entirely to London, though comrades from Liverpool occasionally came down to the capital when they could scrape together the rail fare. The group was so weak, however, that meetings frequently had to be abandoned because there was not even a quorum. The Grantites were in a sorry state.

After the break-up of the RCP, Gerry Healy's group had kept the Fourth International franchise, but in 1953 the Fourth International split, and Healy went with a separate international grouping. For three years the Fourth International searched for a new British franchise. (The story goes that it advertised in *Tribune*.) Eventually Grant and his handful of comrades were to get the job, and they set up a new Revolutionary Socialist League (RSL). In return for the official franchise, the RSL agreed to publish English versions of Fourth International documents in their new magazine, *Workers' International Review*. This latest Grant journal first appeared in September 1956, came out regularly every two months for the next year and was published by the RSL under the business name Workers' International Review (Publishers). Today one of Militant's two limited companies, WIR Publications Limited, is the successor to that firm. One issue of *Workers' International Review* contained a letter from another Marxist group operating inside the Labour Party, the Socialist Workers' Federation (SWF). It called on all revolutionary groups to unite on a common programme which would include 'the rejection of the parliamentary "peaceful" road' and would affirm that Parliament was to be used 'merely as a sounding-board'. The letter was signed by the National Secretary of the SWF, Eric S. Heffer.[19]

In 1958 *Workers' International Review* gave way to a new RSL magazine, *Fourth International*. This continued sporadically until 1962.

Even though the RSL had the official Fourth International franchise, it made no significant progress during this period of rapidly rising economic prosperity. Good opportunities were missed. The events in Hungary in 1956 presented British Trotskyists with one such chance, as thousands left the Communist Party. Gerry Healy seized this opportunity, and his Socialist Labour League grew in numbers, becoming an important group within the Labour Party's Young Socialists. But the RSL remained small, insignificant and unappealing. Ted Grant did approach several ex-Communists personally to ask them to join the RSL, but with little success. On one occasion he even went to see Frank Chapple of the electricians' union, who had just left the Communist Party. Chapple says he wrote a few articles for Grant's publications but never became an RSL member.[20]

By the end of the decade the RSL was at a very low ebb. In the light of the increasing success of Gerry Healy and his new Socialist Labour League, some RSL members wanted to pull out of the Labour Party, but in an RSL pamphlet published in 1959, 'Problems of Entrism', Grant rejected the idea of leaving the party:

> It is true that the conditions for entry, as Trotsky outlined them, are still not present. But it would be the height of stupidity to abandon work in the LP [Labour Party] now and launch into 'independent' adventures after a decade or more of work there.... We have to establish ourselves as a tendency in the Labour Movement.[21]

Today, after three decades of work inside the party, Grant's now-established tendency gives the same pamphlet to new members of Militant 'to cut their teeth on'.[22]

In 1958 Ted Grant and Jimmy Deane began a monthly newspaper, *Socialist Fight*. This was the real forerunner of the modern *Militant* and indeed was acknowledged as such by *Militant* in 1970.[23] A four-page broadsheet, it was designed to appeal to workers and ordinary Labour Party members, not just committed Trotskyists. By this time the name Revolutionary Socialist League was being used only internally, and *Socialist Fight* never mentioned the RSL, presumably to avoid the kind of Labour Party discipline meted out against Gerry Healy's Socialist Labour League, which was proscribed in 1959. *Socialist Fight* was nevertheless an RSL paper. In the first issue in January 1958, alongside an article from Grant entitled 'Slump this Year', was a piece on the Young Socialists by Pat (Paddy) Wall.[24] A later contributor to 'Socialist Fight' was Peter Taaffe.[25] Every issue of the paper advertised the Liverpool youth paper *Rally*, and similarly *Rally* in this period always advertised *Socialist Fight*.

In 1962 *Rally* agreed to amalgamate with another, London-based, Young Socialist paper, *Rebel*, produced by Tony Cliff's faction. The resulting journal was called *Young Guard*. But soon the Cliff supporters in *Young Guard*, who included Gus MacDonald (now of Granada Television) and John Palmer (formerly of the *Guardian*), got the upper hand and rejected the *Rally* group's call for a youth charter. Within a few months the Liverpool people left, and for a few months they published yet another journal, *Youth for Socialism*, based in Garston in Liverpool, but this only lasted for four issues.

By 1963, after thirteen years of little success, Grant had done far worse than either of his rivals from RCP days, Gerry Healy and Tony Cliff, who both had strong groups, if only within the youth section of the Labour Party. The Grant group was still small. Its magazines were irregular and badly produced, and 200 miles separated one section in Liverpool from the other in London. On the eve of Labour's return to Government in 1964, these weak components were to form a newspaper which would become the public front of the Militant tendency.

3

Enter Militant

It was a Saturday afternoon early in 1964. A prominent
Labour MP and future Cabinet Minister was entertaining a
group of fellow socialists in the back garden of his home in
west London. A parliamentary colleague, John Baird,
Member for Wolverhampton North-East, had brought along
some Marxist friends: Jimmy Deane, Ted Grant, Keith
Dickinson and Peter Taaffe were among them. The comrades
spent the afternoon discussing politics and the principles of
socialism. Suddenly, after Taaffe had made a particularly
perceptive remark, Baird turned to Deane and said: 'You've
got a brilliant young fellow here, Jim.'[1]

According to Deane, it was then that he and Grant realized
that Taaffe was the right man to be editor of the new paper
they were thinking of starting later in the year. It was a
crucial decision. In the years that followed Taaffe was to be
the organizer whom Grant had been lacking since the days
when he had worked in successful co-operation with Jock
Haston in the WIL and the RCP. Jimmy Deane himself,
though able in many ways and a brilliant speaker, had never
really been an adequate replacement for Haston. Deane's job
had frequently taken him abroad, and he spent much of his
time dealing with family problems at home.

At first Grant had not been convinced that a new, regular
paper would work. Not since the days of the RCP had he

managed to sustain a printed journal which came out on schedule, without fail. The man who was convinced that it would be possible was a young Indian, Sinna Mani, who was active in the Young Socialists in south London. Though Mani was a member of the RSL, Grant regarded him with some suspicion, since at one time he had been a member of Healy's Socialist Labour League. The idea was that the new RSL paper should have a broad outlook, extending beyond the narrow doctrines of the RSL and concentrating on the Young Socialists. Mani felt that such a paper could generate sufficient support from Young Socialist branches to keep going. In the early part of 1964 Mani finally persuaded Grant that the idea was workable, and the two made a trip to Liverpool to ask the comrades there for assistance.

The decision to go ahead with publishing *Militant* was taken at a meeting in the summer of 1964, when about twenty-five members of the RSL, together with a few from outside the organization, met for a whole-day conference in a pub in Kennington, in south London. The fiercest argument that day was over the new paper's title. Among the suggestions were *Spark*, *Vanguard* and *Forward*, but these were considered too old-fashioned. Grant wanted to carry on with the name *Socialist Fight*; the others disagreed, mocking him with the charge that his previous publication had really been a 'socialist failure'.

The title eventually agreed on was *The Militant*. The meeting knew that the Trotskyist American Socialist Workers' Party had been producing a regular printed paper with that name since 1928, and they hoped that their new journal would be similarly successful. Grant did not like the name at first: he said it was not socialist enough, but the meeting outvoted him. The new paper's full title was in fact *The Militant—for Youth and Labour*; the extra words were a sign of the spirit behind the new venture and emphasized that it was primarily a paper for the Young Socialists. 'Youth' and

'Labour' represented the merging of two strands. The first, in essence the Taaffe/Dickinson strand, was from Liverpool and had been associated with the paper *Rally*, aimed at 'youth' within the Labour Party; the second strand represented the group associated with Grant and *Socialist Fight*, the paper which had been designed for the rank and file of the Labour movement, not committed Trotskyists, and which the early *Militant* greatly resembled.

Because of the new emphasis on youth, Militant's first Editorial Board was composed almost entirely of members of the Young Socialists. One exception was Grant himself, who became political editor to compensate for the fact that he could not be editor because he was well beyond Young Socialist age.

Grant provided the paper with historical ballast, an almost religious link with the old RCP and ultimately with Trotsky himself. Taaffe, the editor, was the down-to-earth working-class boy from Birkenhead, who had the enthusiasm and youth. Taaffe would eventually show the RSL the key to success within the Labour Party that Grant had never understood—progress through the party's youth movement.

Although he was officially editor, Taaffe had very little to do with the first few issues of *Militant*, which probably explains why for several editions his name was misspelt (with only one 'f').[2] For three months *Militant* was effectively edited by Mani, who was nominally the business manager. Though Mani did belong to Ted Grant's RSL, the main group behind the paper, for the first few months *Militant* did not belong exclusively to the Grant group.

Issue number 1 came out in October 1964, a few days before Harold Wilson became Prime Minister after thirteen years of Conservative government. It cost 6d. (2½p). 'Drive Out the Tories' read the front-page headline, and typically underneath was added, 'But Labour must have socialist policies.[3] 'Our aim is to be the Marxist voice of the Young

47

Socialists and the militants in the labour movement,' the first editorial proclaimed. 'The sacrifice and collection of money among militant workers and Young Socialists has made possible the production of the paper.... Make it the mass journal of militant labour and socialist youth.'[4]

Taaffe's contribution was an article on 'The Mods and Rockers Problem'. Page three contained the first 'Fighting Fund' appeal, with a modest target of £500 (today Militant often raises more than that at a single public meeting). Perhaps emphasizing the Liverpool connection, there was a review of the Beatles' film, *A Hard Day's Night*, by Roger Protz, a recent recruit to the RSL from Healy's Socialist Labour League. Protz had once edited the League's *Keep Left* and was initially responsible for *Militant*'s layout.

Under Mani's brief stewardship the early *Militant* displayed a much greater spirit of tolerance than it has in recent times. 'Signed articles express the views of their authors and not necessarily those of the editorial board,' it declared.[5] And Protz was even able to urge the comrades: 'Let's stop kidding ourselves that capitalism is about to quietly keel over and roll into its grave.' This was hardly the sort of thing to endear him to Grant, though it was also stated that the comments were 'solely those of the author'.[6]

Along with that air of tolerance—quite unlike anything in *Militant* today—was another important development in the RSL. A few days before publication of the first issue of *Militant* the International Secretariat of the Fourth International had persuaded Grant and his comrades to merge with some Marxists from Nottingham, known as the Nottingham Group or the International Group. They too practised entrism and had recently started a journal called *The Week* (only a duplicated publication at first), which was sponsored by several MPs and a trade union official called Jim Mortimer.[7] The merger was agreed one weekend in September 1964, at the end of a conference in Sevenoaks held by the National Association of Labour Student Organizations.

The leaders of the International Group were two former members of the Communist Party, Ken Coates and Pat Jordan, who ran a left-wing bookshop in Nottingham. Coates had long been in touch with Grant, and Jordan had sold both *Socialist Fight* and *Rally* in his shop. The International Secretariat hoped that this merger would strengthen their British group. 'This unification marks a very important step forward for the Trotskyist movement in Britain,' Jimmy Deane wrote at the time.[8]

It was a forced engagement, though, and it never worked. There were no tangible results: both groups carried on producing their own publications, *The Week* and *Militant*. Neither journal ever mentioned the other. A few weeks after the agreement Protz wrote to an RSL member in Scotland:

> Unfortunately factionalism is raising its head with Grant and Co.'s insistence not only that *Militant* should be a 'tendency' paper but that it must also be a 'youth and labour' paper, which adds up to them trying to cut *The Week*'s slender neck.[9]

Not for the last time, Grant wanted to have it all his own way. Later Protz was to write about a *Militant* Editorial Board meeting:

> We told Grant that he was hopelessly factional and sectarian, that his attitude would strangle *Militant* and that he had no right to read anybody else's articles until he had written his own. He began screaming and shouting, threatening that I had no rights at all as I wasn't active in the RSL, hadn't 'proved' myself, etc.[10]

By January 1965 Protz felt that he no longer cared about what happened to *Militant* but that *The Week* should be supported 'to the hilt':

When I arrived for a Militant EB [Editorial Board] last night the Grantites were howling with laughter at the first printed *The Week*—'Look at this, ha, ha—isn't it dreadful? Ho, ho.'[11]

Not surprisingly, it wasn't long before the engagement was broken off. Early in 1965 the International Group became the International Marxist Group (IMG), and *The Week* continued as its paper. Before long the International Secretariat of the Fourth International had disenfranchised Grant and the RSL and had recognized the IMG instead. The young Tariq Ali, a wealthy Oxford undergraduate from Pakistan, who had just joined the IMG, was more their idea of a revolutionary than the ageing Ted Grant. Before their departure a future IMG Secretary remarked: 'Grant and Co. should be put out of the International (they haven't paid a penny in subs for years) because they refuse to accept the politics of a majority and because they are not really a Trotskyist tendency.'[12]

The International Marxist Group stayed inside the Labour Party until 1968. Recently, as the Socialist League, the former IMG has been re-entering the party and in August 1983 achieved considerable publicity when thirteen League members were sacked by BL at Cowley.

One of the original leaders of the IMG, Ken Coates, was expelled from the Labour Party in 1965 for criticizing the Government's economic policy. By the time Coates had regained a party card in 1969, he had left the IMG. Since 1968 Coates has concentrated on running the Institute for Workers' Control, one of the important bodies within the Bennite left, and the Bertrand Russell Peace Foundation, both based in Nottingham. In 1983 Coates stood as Labour candidate in Nottingham South (and lost). His son Laurence, a Militant member, served as Young Socialist representative on the Labour NEC from 1981 to 1983.

After Taaffe had come down to London from Liverpool to

fulfil his duties as editor of *Militant*, Protz and Mani separately broke with Grant and the RSL, though neither joined the IMG. The two men who had done so much to put the first few issues of *Militant* together had lost the battle to keep it a paper with a broad Marxist outlook within the Young Socialists. From that point onwards *Militant* was exclusively the paper of one particular Trotskyist tendency, the RSL. As if to illustrate the partial movement away from the emphasis on 'youth', in May 1965 the subtitle changed from 'for Youth and Labour' to 'for Labour and Youth'.[13] And, for the first time, Peter Taaffe's name was spelt with two 'f's.

Protz later joined Tony Cliff's International Socialists and edited *Socialist Worker*. But perhaps he is best known for his work in the Campaign for Real Ale (CAMRA), in the early 1970s. Unsuccessful in bringing about a political revolution, Protz could at least point to his contribution to the mid-1970s revolution in the quality of British beer. He is now press officer of Islington Council.

As some people were leaving Militant, however, another significant group was emerging. While Liverpool and London had provided the new tendency with two important elements, a third now came from Brighton, based at the new University of Sussex. Two second-year students, Roger Silverman, son of the left-wing Labour MP Sydney Silverman, and Alan Woods from South Wales, had been selling *Militant* from the very first issue. Over the next few years the Sussex comrades were to provide the tendency with much needed financial contributions, but, more important, they were to play a leading role in Militant in the years ahead. Others from Sussex were two members of the present Editorial Board, Lynn Walsh and Clare Doyle, who were both expelled by the Labour Party in 1983; Pat Craven, a future business manager; and Bob Edwards, a Central Committee member. Militant was to remain strong in Brighton throughout the 1960s, and it produced its own Sussex University magazines,

Spark and *International Perspectives*. Another important figure at Sussex was a physics lecturer, Geoff Jones, who provided continuity and an important link with the party in Brighton Kemptown, which was eventually taken over by Militant in the 1970s and chose a Militant member, Rod Fitch, as its parliamentary candidate for the 1983 election.

By early 1965 the modern Militant tendency was becoming recognizable. The RSL was still small—no more than a hundred members—but it was well on the road to what it is today. Three important elements had come together around a single national newspaper, *Militant*: Grant and his colleagues from the RCP, providing the historic link with Trotsky; the Liverpool group, contributing the youth and working-class elements; and the students at Sussex, who would give the tendency an important young, middle-class and intellectual ingredient.

For the first few years of its existence Militant progressed almost unnoticed. Originally offices were rented from a Militant sympathizer at 374 Gray's Inn Road, London, above the Connolly Club. In 1965 Militant moved a few hundred yards, to 197 King's Cross Road, where it rented rooms from the Independent Labour Party, which also lent Militant several thousands of pounds. Ten years later the ILP was repaid when the Brighton Kemptown constituency successfully proposed that the ILP should be allowed to return to the Labour Party as Independent Labour Publications. But Militant was still a tiny organization. Of the initial £500 Fighting Fund target, only £150 was raised in the first year. Some months the paper did not appear, and throughout the 1960s it never expanded beyond four pages. Meetings were badly attended: fifty was considered a good turnout; twenty was average. The only notable supporter of Militant at this time was Ellis Hillman, a member of the Greater London Council and a leading geologist who had long been active in Trotskyist circles. Hillman claims that he never actually joined the RSL, but he wrote for *Militant* and frequently spoke at RSL meetings. 'I was simply being used by them,' he says today.[14]

It was to be several years before Militant made any significant progress within the Labour Party. In 1964 the Gerry Healy faction, around the newspaper *Keep Left*, was in control of the Young Socialists (YS); the Cliff group, around *Young Guard*, was their nearest rival in the YS. The RSL was puny in comparison.

Then, as so often in its past, the Labour Party youth section was going through a period of turmoil and conflict with party officials. The troubles were nothing new, as one historian has commented: 'The history of Labour youth is one of conflict, suppression and constant reorganization.'[15] The problem for more than sixty years has been that party officials see a youth section in purely organizational terms: as a means of recruiting new young members and of providing an enthusiastic workforce at election time. Leaders of successive youth sections have always resented the constitutional restrictions placed upon them and have wanted a larger say in party affairs. Because youth sections have invariably been dominated by the Marxist left, in the form either of orthodox Communists or of Trotskyists, the leadership has been reluctant to grant greater freedom to young socialists. This, in turn, has contributed to the resentment felt by members of the youth section towards the rest of the party.

On three occasions, in 1936, 1940 and 1955, the Labour Party had closed down its youth section at national level because it had been taken over by a Marxist faction that the leadership did not like. In 1960, after Labour's third successive general election defeat, the party once again re-established its national youth section, hoping to win more members and voters among the young. Gradually the new Young Socialists, as they were now called, were taken over by Trotskyists, and the YS conference called on party leader

Hugh Gaitskell to resign. The result was again disciplinary action, instigated by the Assistant National Agent, Reg Underhill. In 1962 and 1963 several *Keep Left* supporters were expelled, and a number of branches were closed down. The factionalism within the YS reached a peak at its Conference in 1964, when the Chairman told delegates he would 'march to socialism over your dead bodies'.[16] He was later expelled.

In 1964 the YS National Conference was abolished for the fourth time, although the National Committee was maintained, now appointed by the party. Individual YS branches continued in the constituencies. The now dominant *Keep Left* faction went ahead and organized its own unofficial YS conference, at which it proclaimed *Keep Left* the YS paper. This meeting marked the departure of *Keep Left* and the Healyites from the Labour Party. The Young Socialists became the official youth section of the Socialist Labour League; and today the youth section of the League's successor, the Workers' Revolutionary Party, still carries the same name, Young Socialists. To avoid confusion, in 1965 the Labour Party youth section became the Labour Party Young Socialists (LPYS).

Shortly afterwards the other major Trotskyist faction within the party's youth section, the Cliff group, around *Young Guard*, also quit the party. So by 1967 the Militant tendency, as it was now becoming known (the name Revolutionary Socialist League was used only internally) was the sole significant Trotskyist group left inside the LPYS. But Militant was still small, and the LPYS was now very weak.

In 1967 the NEC allowed the LPYS National Committee to carry out a review of its organization. The following year the Simpson Committee on Labour Party organization recommended changes in the LPYS which 'would give to the Young Socialists more control of their own organization than the Labour Youth Movement has ever enjoyed before'.[17]

Later the NEC agreed that the LPYS should publish its own newspaper, *Left*, which would for the first time be free from censorship and would have an editor chosen by the LPYS itself. In time *Left* (now called *Socialist Youth*) simply became a poorer version of *Militant*, subsidized by the party.

Disillusionment with the Wilson Government greatly helped Militant's rise. Wilson's support for the Americans in Vietnam, the introduction of incomes policy, the failure to deal with the Smith regime in Rhodesia, conflict with the unions and proposals for anti-union legislation in *In Place of Strife* and, above all, the failure of the Government to live up to the high expectations that had been created largely by Wilson himself, engendered a sense of betrayal. Labour Party membership plummeted. But the strongest reaction was probably that among young people, who were in revolt throughout the Western world. Militant benefited from two, almost contradictory, trends. On the one hand the far left had given up the Labour Party and withdrawn, while the social democratic faction and the right, which had hitherto had some influence within the party's youth section, were totally discredited by the Government's performance.

The way was now open for Militant. The tendency succeeded because nobody else in the LPYS was offering any credible alternative. The first Militant supporter on the National Committee was elected in 1967. By 1969 the LPYS Conference had accepted Militant's 'Charter for Young Workers' (first proposed by *Rally* in 1950), and the following year Militant achieved a majority on the LPYS National Committee. The tendency has retained that majority to this day, virtually unchallenged.

Most young people in the late 1960s regarded the Labour Party as the last place in which to be politically active. It was an era which marked the rise of the single-issue pressure group, and Trotskyist organizations outside the party began to grow. The Vietnam war demonstrations, pop music and pot-smoking of the 1960s generation did not interest Militant, which saw the new culture as a distraction from the real issues. While thousands demonstrated in Grosvenor Square, Militant sought the nationalization of the top 380 monopolies. Militant's growing influence within the LPYS went largely unremarked. Compared with previous generations of Young Socialists, from *Advance!* in the 1930s to *Keep Left* in the early 1960s, Militant was seen as less troublesome. The Young Liberals, protesting about Vietnam and apartheid, were far more of an embarrassment to Jeremy Thorpe at this time than the LPYS was to Harold Wilson. With a National Executive that was moving leftwards, it came as no surprise when the LPYS was rewarded with even more autonomy.

An important advantage for the tendency was that the unions have no involvement in the Labour Party youth section, whereas in the Labour Party itself the unions hold nearly 90 per cent of the Conference votes and have often used this power to offset the leftward inclinations of the constituencies. In the LPYS all the votes come from individual branches.

Branches were the key to success, and taking them over was a simple task for Militant. The first necessary ingredient in Militant's formula is a Militant member within the LPYS branch. If necessary, one is asked to move into a constituency from elsewhere. This is easier if the LPYS branch is a new one, as many were in the late 1960s, when the LPYS was being revived. The Militant member sells copies of the paper to other LPYS members and at an early stage suggests a programme of Militant speakers. These speakers will be presented not as being from Militant but as experts on particular subjects, such as Chile or Spain. After a few weeks' work in a branch the key Militant member will assess its prospects. If further recruits look likely and takeover seems possible, then the other LPYS members will slowly be drawn into the tendency. But if other groups are strong and a takeover looks difficult, then the Militant member may abandon the struggle in that particular branch. He or she will stop going to meetings and may move elsewhere. In some cases, where control looks out of reach, Militant may try to smash the branch altogether so as to stop it from falling into the hands of others. A common Militant tactic is to hold LPYS branch meetings as regularly as possible. In this way many of the non-Militant members find that because of other commitments—homework, girl- or boyfriends or families— they are unable to attend every meeting. This only strengthens the position of the disciplined Militant members who, of course, go to every meeting. Once Militant is entrenched in an LPYS branch, non-Militant members will often feel unwelcome and will stop going. LPYS weekend and summer schools are used regularly by Militant as a means of establishing contact with branches they have not taken over yet and for finding and developing new sympathizers.

In 1969 the Labour Party appointed a full-time National Youth Officer, Neil Vann. Vann was an energetic former constituency agent who genuinely wanted the party to have a strong youth section, but he quickly found that he was spending most of his energy battling against Militant, with very little support from his superiors. 'It was a matter all the time of sticking your finger into holes in the dyke', he recalls.[18] Vann did all he could to encourage non-Militant LPYS members, but it was an uphill task. Many party members of LPYS age ignored the youth section, and many of those who did get involved in the LPYS had other commitments in local Labour parties and student politics which distracted them. Nobody could ever match Militant's dedication. Vann remembers that even before Militant had a majority on the LPYS National Committee, the non-Militant members could never count on outvoting them: 'While all the five Militant supporters would always turn up, it was always in doubt whether the non-Militants would. They often didn't have the time. They'd be local councillors or fully entrenched in other work in the Labour Party.'[19] When Vann started as National Youth Officer, the LPYS National Committee held a three-hour meeting every two months. But once Militant took control the meetings were held monthly and lasted from early on Saturday afternoon to Sunday lunchtime. 'And the annoying thing about it was that they had all met together beforehand anyway', he remembers.[20]

After 1970, when Militant controlled the National Committee, only one region, the West Midlands, stood out against the tendency, thanks partly to the work of the Assistant Regional Organizer. (The region was to remain outside Militant hands until 1975 and was not totally secure after that.) The 1970 takeover of the LPYS marked a real turning-point in the tendency's fortunes. Thereafter membership climbed rapidly, since the LPYS was an excellent source of recruits, funds and some power. In effect the LPYS became a section not of the Labour Party but of the Militant tendency, and Militant treated the finances almost as if they were integrated. Militant also found the party youth section a good training ground. LPYS National Committees from the early 1970s consisted almost entirely of people who today, a decade later, are full-time workers for Militant. And control of hundreds of LPYS branches gave the tendency a foothold in nearly every constituency. An LPYS branch is entitled to at least two delegates on the General Committee of a constituency Labour party and can also submit resolutions to the Committee. The fact that many branches consist of a mere handful of members goes largely unnoticed in the rest of the party. The LPYS manages to carry on with between 5,000 and 10,000 members nationally. Most non-Militant Labour Party members between the ages of 15 and 25 end up ignoring the LPYS and concentrate on the party itself.

In 1972 the party made another concession to the youth section—a place on the NEC for a representative from the LPYS. This move gave Militant an important position within Transport House, and not just a voice and a vote in the party's most important body but ears as well. The left on the NEC was to find the LPYS representative a useful ally. In return for his support in battles against the right, the left would defend the LPYS and Militant. Successive Militant members on the NEC were able to keep the Militant leadership informed of every move inside Labour headquarters, and Peter Taaffe and Ted Grant now had direct access to confidential documents distributed to NEC members. In time journalists too were to find the LPYS NEC member a useful contact.

Almost continuously since 1972 the NEC place has been held by a Militant supporter: Peter Doyle, Nick Bradley, Tony Saunois, Laurence Coates and, at the moment, Steve Morgan. The only period when Militant did not hold the position was for six months in 1974, after Peter Doyle was forced to resign. It was suddenly discovered that Doyle was 27, two years over-age. One of Militant's few opponents within the LPYS had long suspected this and had eventually gone to Somerset House to dig out a copy of Doyle's birth certificate. Doyle's replacement on the NEC was Rose Degiorgio, a non-Militant candidate who had received just seventeen votes at the 1973 LPYS Conference (as opposed to 141 for Doyle). Rarely can anybody have found him- or herself elevated to the NEC with so little support or in such unusual circumstances.

In 1970 Militant bought its own offices in Bethnal Green in east London, and members of the tendency were dragooned into decorating the building and reconstructing the drains. Then Militant bought its own press; until that time the paper had been produced by a friendly printer in a basement in Fulham. As a result *Militant* quickly changed from a 'skimpy monthly' into a 'lively weekly'[21] and extended from four pages to eight. And it started to sport a colour logo too, though it has always been more orange than red. Many of the organizational advances within the tendency were the work of Dave Galashan, Militant's business manager, who had known Peter Taaffe since his days in Liverpool. Galashan masterminded Militant's finances, ran the business side of the newspaper and organized Militant's printing work. He eventually left Militant at the end of the 1970s, exhausted by his work. Today he works as an audio engineer for the BBC but is still loyal to Militant. The jobs Galashan did are now carried out by several different people.

During the period of the Heath Government, Militant's style of politics—concentrating on economic and industrial issues—began to have more appeal. The Campaign for Nuclear Disarmament and Vietnam protesters who had marched down Whitehall in the 1950s and 1960s gave way to demonstrators angry about the Industrial Relations Act, the Pentonville Five, Upper Clyde Shipbuilders, the Shrewsbury Pickets and the Clay Cross councillors. It was a period of great industrial unrest. On five occasions in less than four years the Heath Government had to proclaim a State of Emergency. More days were lost through industrial disputes than in any comparable period since records began, and Britain saw the miners on strike for the first time since 1926—not once but twice. The tendency exploited these conflicts and disputes to the full. *Militant*-sellers began to be a common feature of the picket lines, and the newspaper expanded its coverage of industrial affairs. By 1974 the tendency had around 500 members,[22] compared with just over 100 four years before.

Soon Militant began to make an impact on the wider Labour Party. At the 1972 Conference in Blackpool Pat Wall, the delegate from Shipley, and Ray Apps, from Brighton Kemptown, proposed a composite motion calling for 'an enabling Bill to secure the public ownership of major monopolies', a watered-down version of Militant's main policy. The Conference, largely unaware that both delegates were members of the Militant National Committee or probably even what Militant was, passed it by 3,501,000 votes to 2,497,000.[23] It was quite an achievement. The fact that Wall and Apps were able to make sure that it was they who were chosen to propose the composite resolution which amalgamated several constituency motions, showed that there had been considerable planning by Militant beforehand. The following year similar co-ordination was less successful. A Militant motion proposed by Brighton Kemptown and Liverpool Walton, calling for the nationalization of 250 monopolies, was defeated overwhelmingly.[24] This period also saw the first attempts by Militant members to secure election to the NEC. The early results were promising: 31,000 votes for Ray Apps in 1971; 51,000 for Militant's business manager, Pat Craven, in 1972; and in 1973 81,000 for Apps and 144,000 for David Skinner (brother of the MP, Dennis Skinner),[25] whose vote was boosted because he was one of the Clay Cross councillors who had been disqualified from council office for defying the Housing Finance Act. For the first time Militant members secured more votes than any other candidate who was not an MP. Even though Militant candidates were less successful in many subsequent years, they have nearly always done better than any other non-parliamentary candidates (see Appendix 1).

It would be wrong, however, to deduce that these rising votes automatically represented growing support for Militant in the constituencies. Each local party has 1,000 votes in the constituency ballot (more in the rare case of a party with over 1,000 members) and can vote for seven candidates. But the 81,000 votes for Ray Apps in 1973 did not necessarily mean that eighty-one constituency parties then supported Militant. At that time the mandating of Conference delegates on who to vote for was less common than today. The choice was often left to the delegate, and in many parties Militant supporters found it easy to get chosen as delegates (in some cases nobody else volunteered). Where delegates were mandated there was nothing to stop them from breaking the mandates, as the ballot was secret until 1983, when (significantly) Militant withdrew at the last minute. But, above all, in the early 1970s Militant did not suffer the kind of counter-reaction it meets today. Pat Wall could never get his 1972 motion through Conference now, simply because he and several of his colleagues are publicly identified as members of Militant.

An internal Militant document published in June 1974 boasted that the tendency had 'extended and given a new dimension to Trotsky's conception of entry'.[26] But for the first decade of its entrism Militant had worked largely unobserved within the Labour Party, swiftly taking over the Young Socialists and establishing a foothold in the wider party. Militant had briefly made a minor attempt at entrism within the Communist Party as well in the early 1970s but, not surprisingly, Communist leaders were more aware, and less tolerant, of Militant than were those of the Labour Party. As Peter Taaffe and Ted Grant celebrated *Militant*'s tenth birthday in October 1974, they did have much to be proud of, but they had also been fortunate. Now they would have to use the gains made in the LPYS as a basis for advances elsewhere: 'The Constituency Parties are assuming more and more importance for our work,' the document stated.[27] 'We must dig roots in the wards and constituencies as we have in the YS. Many are still shells dominated by politically dead old men and women.'[28] But when these plans were later carried out, they were met with increasing opposition.

4

Policies and Programme

For most people in politics 'slogan' is a pejorative term, often used to condemn the propaganda of opponents. Militant, however, happily admits that slogans are an important part of its political strategy. According to Militant's leading economic thinker, Andrew Glyn: '*Militant* campaigns for a socialist programme summarized in the slogan: "Nationalize the 200 monopolies and the banks under workers' control and management, and with compensation according to proven need".'[1]

The 'Nationalize the 200 monopolies' demand is the most important of several simple slogans used by the tendency. Others include '£100 a week minimum wage' and 'Thirty-five hour week without loss of pay'. These demands can be found throughout Militant's literature and Militant resolutions to local Labour parties or party Conference can often be identified by them. Most of the other important Militant slogans are among the tendency's list of basic demands, set out at the start of the pamphlet 'Militant: What We Stand For', written by Peter Taaffe in 1981 (the numbering is mine):

1. The immediate introduction of a thirty-five-hour week without loss in pay as a step towards the elimination of unemployment.

63

2. Reversal of all Tory cuts and a massive programme of public works on housing, education, the health service etc.

3. A minimum wage of £90 [now £100] a week, including for the pensioners, the sick and disabled.

4. Opposition to the Tory Government's anti-union bill and reversal of all attacks on the trade unions.

5. Workers' management of the nationalized industries on the basis of one-third of the places on the management board coming from the unions in the industry, one-third from the TUC representing the working class as a whole and one-third from the Government.

6. Nationalization under workers' control and management of all firms threatening redundancies.

7. Opening of the books of the monopolies to inspection by committees of shop stewards, housewives and small shop-keepers.

8. Opposition to racism and fascism and all racist immigration laws, particularly the Tory Government's racist Nationality Act. We also recognize that only by unifying black and white workers in a struggle for socialist change can racism and fascism be effectively abolished.

9. Opposition to discrimination on the basis of sex. We call for equal pay for work of equal value, for a crash programme to build nurseries, schools, etc.

10. Total opposition to the dictatorship of the Fleet Street Press who pour out their poison daily against the labour movement. We propose that a Labour Government should nationalize the newspaper printing plant facilities, radio and TV. Access to these facilities should be given to political parties, in proportion to their votes at elections.

11. Abolition of the monarchy and House of Lords.

12. Nationalization of the top 200 monopolies, including the banks and insurance companies which control the 'commanding heights' of the economy through an Enabling Bill in Parliament with minimum compensation

on the basis of proven need. This would then allow a socialist plan of production to be democratically drawn up and
implemented by committees involving the trade unions,
shop stewards, housewives and small businessmen.

13. For a twenty-four-hour general strike to be organized
by the TUC against Tory cuts and Tebbit's anti-union Bill.
This to be part of a campaign to force a general election
and bring a Labour Government to power on a socialist
programme.

14. Opposition to the capitalist Common Market. For a
Socialist United States of Europe as a step towards a World
Socialist Federation.

15. Massive cuts in arms spending. . . . Support for unilateral nuclear disarmament, but with the recognition that
only a socialist change of society in Britain and inter-
nationally can eliminate the danger of a nuclear holocaust.

16. Defence of mandatory reselection of MPs.

17. Election of a Labour Cabinet/Shadow Cabinet by the
electoral college.

18. NEC control of the election Manifesto, based on Party
conference decisions.

19. All Labour MPs to receive the average wage of a skilled
worker plus expenses; the surplus to be given to the labour
movement.[2]

Of the above demands, only points 2, 4, 8, 9 and 16 are
Labour Party policy as agreed by party Conference.

Interestingly, in the period since Taaffe wrote his
pamphlet several of the above demands have disappeared
from the list, which is now published regularly in *Militant*.
The nationalization of firms threatening redundancies, the
opening of the books of the monopolies, the call for a twenty-
four-hour TUC general strike and the abolition of the
monarchy and the House of Lords have been forgotten,
presumably so that Militant will not be seen as too extreme—

Militant's demand for abolition of the monarchy is frequently quoted against it in the popular press. Demands 16 to 19, on Labour Party democracy, have also fallen by the wayside.

To discover the origins of Militant's policies we have to go back to the Transitional Programme drawn up by Trotsky for the founding conference of the Fourth International in 1938. Trotsky wrote:

> It is necessary to help the masses in the process of the daily struggle to find the bridge between present demands and the socialist programme of the revolution. The bridge should include a system of transitional demands, stemming from today's conditions and from today's consciousness of wide layers of the working class and unalterably leading to one final conclusion: the conquest of power by the proletariat.[3]

Militant's main economic thinker, Andrew Glyn, is a tutor at Corpus Christi College, Oxford, whom Grant and Taaffe see regularly. He explains how the interests of the working class can be safeguarded only by campaigns around slogans: 'The struggle for these demands by the organizations of the labour movement immediately raises the question of whether workers' basic requirements can be guaranteed under capitalism, and the corresponding need to generalize these struggles around a programme to transform society.'[4] Militant's demands are simple policies, which are easily memorable and designed to appeal to the working class. They are meant to appear reasonable under existing conditions. Militant's programme is simply a list of modern-day 'transitional demands', which have been updated since 1938. Peter Taaffe's 1981 pamphlet can be seen as a new version of Trotsky's Transitional Programme. Several of Militant's demands—opening the books of the monopolies and the programme of public works—have remained almost unaltered since Trotsky's day.

But it is essential to understand that for Militant the implementation of these transitional demands is far less important than their use as a means by which to raise the political consciousness of the advanced elements of the working class. The transitional demands are a reasonable bait to make Militant attractive to workers or left-wing trade unionists who have become disillusioned with traditional Labour policies and are now 'reaching out for the ideas of revolutionary Marxism'. Once the new 'contact member' has been drawn into the tendency, all will be revealed to him or her. A careful programme of education is constructed to raise further the consciousness of the new member, who is given the basic texts to read, among them the *Transitional Programme*, *Where is Britain Going?* and the *History of the Russian Revolution*, all by Trotsky, and a collection of his works on entrism, together with Marx's *Communist Manifesto*. These are the main works upon which Militant's true organization, policy and programme are based. Ideally, every new member has to read and understand them; in practice nowadays this may not always happen. For Militant parliamentary democracy is not important. True, Militant has now got two of its members elected to parliament, but this is seen only as a step in raising workers' consciousness and in the process towards revolution.

In the late 1930s Trotsky believed capitalism was going through its 'death agony'. Whether Trotsky would have continued to believe that in the years since then is debatable, but Militant has certainly stuck with Trotsky's view. 'Capitalism is condemned. Nothing will save it from collapse,' Trotsky wrote then, though these words might as well have been written by Grant or Taaffe at any time since. After the war Ted Grant faithfully carried on believing that capitalism's collapse was near, even during the post-war boom and in the face of economic indicators which suggested that the Western economy was thriving far more than in Trotsky's day. Unlike other Trotskyist groups, though, Militant has never insisted that the collapse will happen immediately—only that the pre-revolutionary situation will be evident in the 'coming period' (ten or fifteen years away perhaps). Like so many other Trotskyist groups, Militant is optimistic about the collapse of capitalism; its optimism increases as the world economy suffers worse troubles. In the 1960s Militant asked, 'Will there be a slump?', but in recent times the question has become 'Will there be a boom?' For Militant sees the world depression of the last ten years as a vindication of what its arguments were in the 1950s and 1960s.

Alongside Militant's thesis that world capitalism is in decline is the claim that in Britain the capitalist crisis is even more severe than elsewhere. 'The whole of British society is heading for a gigantic explosion,' Grant wrote in 1973.[5] To support this view the tendency's publications will quote from the pages of right-wing journals such as the *Financial Times*, the *Banker* and *Management Today*: Britain's declining share of world trade and output, its low growth rate since the war compared with that of other countries, the failure of British companies to invest and the falling value of the pound against foreign currencies. According to Peter Taaffe, the 'long economic upswing' that marked the period 1950–75 is now over. The only way to avoid the 'calamity that looms in the next decade', he says, is to replace capitalism with a 'socialist Britain and a socialist plan of production',[6] which would centre on nationalization of the companies which control the economy.

Another important theme of Militant's ideology is that of the constant betrayal of the working class by its leaders— from Ramsay MacDonald to the right-wing and left-wing 'reformists' of recent times: Wilson, Callaghan, Foot and ultimately Kinnock among the politicians and, of course, most trade union leaders. Militant argues that Labour Governments, past and future, inevitably foster working-class disillusionment with their leadership. If another Labour Government were ever elected, it is inevitable, according to Militant, that its 'reformist' policies would fail because of the pressures of capitalism, and this would only deepen the despair of ordinary workers. All this would happen against the backdrop of the 'crisis of international capitalism'.

Eventually circumstances will worsen, so Militant argues, and there will be food riots, industrial unrest, armed police and soldiers on the picket lines, the collapse of law and order and deteriorating conditions for working people. On top of that Militant expects an increasingly ineffectual Government in Whitehall, be it Conservative or, more likely, 'reformist Labour'. With the working class effectively leaderless, the theory is that the tendency's long-term preparation will equip it perfectly with its 'vanguard of cadres', to assume the leadership of the labour movement. The whole of Militant's present strategy is to prepare for that moment, recruiting people to the tendency and training them to be part of the revolutionary vanguard. Work inside the Labour Party is used only as a means of making that task easier. It is Militant's aim not simply to take the party over but to prepare to assume the leadership of the working class.

Once Militant has assumed that leadership, during a period of economic crisis, it will try to form workers' councils, workers' militias and, if necessary, a provisional Government. The model for this programme of events is, of course, the Russian Revolution in 1917, which Militant often says was the most important event in world history.

Publicly Militant always argues that when the time comes for the final transition from capitalism to socialism, the power of the labour and trade union movement will be such as to ensure that it happens without violence. Even so, Militant constantly quotes the example of Chile and insists that this reveals the possibility of violence on the part of the 'capitalist class' in defence of what it sees as its right to rule.

Militant's thesis is that a future left-wing reformist Labour Government might find itself in a position similar to that of the democratically elected Government of Salvador Allende in Chile in 1973—a left 'reformist' Goverment which was overthrown by the CIA. The tendency believes that Allende could have prevented what happened by arming the workers in Chile, and it argues that if similar circumstances arose in Britain, armed workers' militias should be established solely for defensive purposes at a time when 'capitalists' would be trying to overthrow a Labour Government: in theory violence would be invoked only to counter-attack. Militant insists publicly that it does not preach violent revolution, but it would have no hesitation in using violence in defence of the working class. In such circumstances it might become difficult to determine who had used violence first and to define what was meant by violence.

Once violence from the right had been successfully suppressed, then stronger measures would undoubtedly be introduced. In Pat Wall's words: 'It would mean the abolition of the monarchy, the House of Lords, the sacking of the generals, the admirals, the air marshals, the senior civil servants, the police chiefs and in particular, the judges and people of that character.'[7] In time, Parliament would be superseded by workers' councils or soviets, and political parties found to be giving support to the 'forces of capitalism' would be outlawed, including possibly the Labour Party itself. The trade unions too might not survive: 'We must never forget to train our cadres to the theoretical possibility of the unions as organizations being thrust aside, in a period of revolution or prior to an insurrection, and that workers committees or soviets could take their place.'[8]

Little of Militant's revolutionary plan is stated explicitly by the tendency, even in its secret internal documents, but it is exactly in line with the teachings of Marx, Engels, Lenin and Trotsky. Peter Taaffe undoubtedly sees himself as the modern British Lenin who will take over at the moment of crisis and lead us to socialism.

What that socialism would eventually entail is unclear. According to Marx's *Communist Manifesto*, private property would be abolished, and society would be administered by the workers through workers' councils. There would be no role for political parties, for Parliament as we know it or probably even for trade unions. Eventually, Marx believed, the state would wither away, and we would be left with a land of 'undreamed-of plenty' with none of the evils of capitalism, as Alan Woods and Ted Grant put it:

> The nightmare of Stalinism and capitalism will become bad memories of the past, and the blossoming of the productive forces of the planet, integrated under a system of democratic control and planning, will enable art, culture and science to rise to unheard of levels. For the first time, Man will be able to draw himself up to his true stature in a world freed from wars, poverty and oppression.[9]

Since Militant's public programme is 'transitional' and designed solely as a method of increasing workers' consciousness, any attempt to argue with it becomes a fairly pointless exercise. Militant's public programme disguises the tendency's fundamental beliefs. People on the left frequently assert that Militant should be countered by political argument, but it is not as simple as that. Militant's true programme and policies are never openly stated. The items in its public programme have not been designed for implementation, at least not by a Militant Government. Any confrontation would be a bit like being drawn against Everton in a cup match and finding, when you get to the ground, that you are playing Liverpool.

One consequence of Militant's simple revolutionary programme and grand strategy is that it sees policies put forward by the Labour left as irrelevant to the achievement of social-

71

ism and as distractions. For Militant it is important not to be seen to be too closely associated with left reformists, such as the Bennites, if one day the working class is to reject such 'reformism' and turn to a revolutionary programme. So the Tribunite Alternative Economic Strategy (AES), which has recently become Labour Party and TUC policy, is rejected totally by Militant. Import controls, one of the main planks of the AES, are rejected as 'nationalistic', open to retaliation and simply a matter of exporting unemployment. Most of the other measures of the AES—industrial democracy, planning agreements, a wealth tax and a certain amount of nationalization—are seen by Militant as not going far enough and as an 'attempt to implant in a partial fashion aspects of a full-blooded socialist plan in what would remain fundamentally a capitalist organism'.[10]

But the AES is not the only area where Militant is out of step with the rest of the Labour left. A common charge against the tendency is that of 'economism': Militant is accused of reducing all political issues to economics. It regards activity on single issues, such as peace, as futile unless linked to an 'overall socialist programme'. Militant has refused to join many of the important single-issue campaigns of the left in recent years. In the late 1970s the tendency shunned the Anti-Nazi League because it was run by the Socialist Workers' Party, in spite of the fact that most people agreed the Anti-Nazi League had been quite successful in the fight against the National Front. Often Militant has preferred to set up its own organizations rather than join other pressure groups. The tendency rejected the Right to Work Campaign and instead began its own Youth Opportunities Programme Trade Union Rights Campaign, officially run by the LPYS. Militant controlled it and found it a good source of recruits. Earlier the tendency formed the Youth Campaign Against Unemployment rather than join the wider Campaign Against Youth Unemployment, which had been initiated by the

Young Communist League but which also involved a wide range of other groups. The Labour Abortion Rights Campaign was ignored until it had received official TUC support. As for democratic reforms within the Labour Party, for many years Militant preferred to campaign on its own rather than through the Campaign for Labour Party Democracy. Militant will initiate its own single-issue campaigns only when they become important matters within the labour movement and hence other means of recruiting people to the tendency and raising 'workers' consciousness'.

Until recently Militant adopted a very supercilious attitude to the Campaign for Nuclear Disarmament (CND), which it regarded as for 'vicars and liberals'. Militant dislikes CND's middle-class composition and the Campaign's belief that nuclear disarmament is possible without the election of a Labour Government. But Militant was also much less concerned about the possibility of nuclear war than others on the left:

> The capitalists do not wage war for the sake of waging war but in order to extend their power, income and profit. . . . To destroy the working class, which nuclear war would mean, would be to destroy the goose that lays the golden eggs. . . . Consequently it is only totalitarian fascist regimes, completely desperate and unbalanced, which would take this road.[11]

Peter Taaffe argued in 1978 that 'a war between Russia and the capitalist West is completely ruled out in the foreseeable future.'[12]

But with the growth of the peace movement in recent years Militant has had to modify its views. It had to join the peace movement simply so as not to become discredited within the Labour Party and among members of the Young Socialists. Officially Militant has always believed in unilateral nuclear disarmament and in withdrawal from NATO, but neither has ever been seen as important in the 'struggle for socialism'. It was not until very recently that Militant joined in the activities of Youth CND. In 1983 Militant suddenly realized that Youth CND could be a potential source of new recruits. Shortly after this move Youth CND was closed down by the CND National Committee because of 'infiltration' by groups on the far left. Ironically, two smaller Trotskyist groups—the Socialist League (formerly the International Marxist Group) and the *Socialist Organizer* group—had taken advantage of Youth CND first.

As a Trotskyist faction, Militant is naturally highly critical of the Soviet Union and regards it as a 'degenerated workers' state'. The tendency does believe, however, that the Eastern bloc illustrates the benefits of a planned economy. Militant gives its strong support to the banned trade union Solidarity in Poland and, unlike some on the left such as Arthur Scargill, believes that members of Solidarity are genuine socialists, wanting workers' control in Poland, not a return to capitalism. However, Militant has been fiercely criticized by other Trotskyist groups for its attitude to the Soviet occupation of Afghanistan. While it condemned the occupation by the Soviet Union in 1979, it does not now call for a Soviet withdrawal. In Militant's view, this would mean only a return to the previous 'feudal' society in Afghanistan and would leave the country open to American influence.

Similarly in 1982 Militant took a very unusual line on the Falklands. Though the tendency opposed the war, it did not urge the recall of the Task Force, as did other groups on the left: 'Instead of putting the position in class terms, some lefts and the pacifist wing of the Labour Party put forward the demand "Bring back the Fleet". Such a demand is completely unrealistic and futile.'[13] Ted Grant thought the Falklands conflict could be used to force a general election which could lead to the return of a Labour Government and the formation of a 'socialist federation of Britain, Argentina and the Falk-

74

lands [which] could then bring enormous benefits to the people of both countries'.[14]

Militant has taken an odd position on many of the other major issues for the new left. On Ireland, for instance, it prefers to adapt its formula for the coming British revolution. The tendency believes in a socialist united Ireland and in the withdrawal of British troops but considers that these should be replaced by militias based on the Northern Ireland trade unions: 'This mass force, mobilized in action against sectarianism through a defence force based on trade unions, could do what the army could never do: protect the working class from the bigots of all sides.'[15] Unlike many on the far left Militant is not prepared to condone or to remain silent about acts of terrorism by the IRA, the INLA or other sectarian groups. Militant's formula for bringing peace to Ireland, workers' militias, is put forward as a solution to many of the other of the world's disputes, such as those of the Middle East.

The feminist movement is regarded by Militant as 'petty-bourgeois-dominated' and subject to 'hysteria',[16] though financial expediency does not stop the Militant presses from printing feminist or lesbian newspapers for others. Militant is often very sexist. In Militant cartoons women are often portrayed in an inferior role to men, and workers are always boiler-suited, tough-looking males. Within its own ranks there are very few women in important positions; only about 10 per cent of the tendency's full-timers are female. Recently, however, Militant bowed to the growing mood among its members and set up a women's group.

The tendency regards all social issues essentially as problems of capitalism. Homosexuality is a problem which will disappear under socialism. Gay members of Militant generally keep quiet. The issue of gay rights has only once been raised at the LPYS National Conference since Militant took over the Labour youth section in 1970 (not that it is raised at the Labour Party Conference much either). Militant sees the matter of gay rights as a 'petty-bourgeois diversion', but often members of Militant are hostile to gays. A few years ago, at a British Youth Council reception for some visitors from an East European country, Militant members of the LPYS were seen eagerly quizzing the foreign guests about their country's electric shock treatment for homosexuals.

Militant often requires a highly puritanical lifestyle from its members. Short hair and ties are common, and members are expected to get to bed early at Militant and LPYS summer camps and conferences. When the new Parliament met in 1983 one sketch writer pointed out that the new Militant members could easily be spotted because they were so smartly dressed. The worst crime in Militant's eyes is to indulge in drugs, a 'petty-bourgeois deviation' liable to 'corrupt' working-class people and to 'numb their consciousness'. In Edinburgh three Militant members were once expelled for smoking cannabis. At the 1983 LPYS summer camp the National Committee immediately informed new recruits who supported Militant that there were some bad 'petty-bourgeois' elements at the camp who might be smoking 'substances which could distract them from the real task of transforming society'. But the warning had an unwanted effect—having been told this, the new Militant members went round looking for the strange 'substances'.

Militant manages to see each political development within the Labour Party as justifying its 'perspectives'. In the 1970s Militant's constant prediction was that the right-wingers— the Neanderthal men—would break away, leaving the Tribunites as the dominant force within the party. Militant would then assume the Tribunites' role as the party's left opposition. To some extent Militant's thesis has been proved correct, though fewer right-wingers defected than it had expected. But rather than becoming the party establishment, what has happened is that the Tribunites themselves have split. The soft left—Michael Foot and Neil Kinnock—have become the establishment and have united with those right-wingers who have stayed (such as Roy Hattersley and Peter Shore). The rest of the Tribunites, around Tony Benn, have become the effective opposition, with the allegiance of a whole range of other far-left groups, of which Militant is only one.

It is important to understand that Militant's policies and programme are not just a more radical version of the new left-wing Labour Party manifesto. Militant is not merely a more fervent type of Labour Co-ordinating Committee. The demand to nationalize the top 200 monopolies is more than a more radical form of the long-standing Tribunite demand to take the top twenty-five companies into public ownership. Militant is committed to revolutionary change and believes that change cannot be achieved through parliamentary democracy: internally the tendency is, after all, called the *Revolutionary* Socialist League.

At its mass rally at Wembley in September 1983 Militant displayed two huge red banners behind the platform. On one of them were Engels and Marx; on the other, Lenin and Trotsky. At no point has Militant ever repudiated these four thinkers on any issue. Only those who are naive can believe that they were displayed purely for show or that Militant turns to them for nothing more than simple inspiration. Militant believes in the kind of revolution carried out by Lenin and Trotsky in the Soviet Union but without the Stalinist stage that followed. Revolution in Britain would lead to revolution throughout the world.

Tony Benn has defended Militant by arguing that Marxism has always been a 'legitimate strand of thought' within the Labour Party. He misses the point. Militant is not just Marxist but also Leninist and Trotskyist; as a result it has a style of secretive and disciplined politics that is wholly alien to the democratic traditions of the Labour Party.

77

5

Operation Icepick

Five days before Christmas 1976, a fifty-two-seater coach sped south down the M6 on its way from Scotland to Lancaster. Most people travelling north along the motorway that afternoon probably would not have noticed it: the vehicle was just one of hundreds of coaches you pass on any long motorway journey. But more observant drivers, glancing across the central reservation at the oncoming traffic, might just have spotted that on the front of this particular vehicle, tied by wire to the radiator grille, was a brand-new icepick.

The 'Icepick Express' was not carrying a party of mountaineers back from a climbing weekend in the Cairngorms. On board, in fact, were nearly fifty Scottish students on their way to the 1976 Conference of the National Organization of Labour Students (NOLS) at Lancaster University, all of them sworn enemies of Trotskyism and of Militant in particular. They were going to Lancaster determined to stop Militant from regaining power in NOLS. When the coach left Glasgow the party on board had included a rather lonely band of Militant supporters. But when the party stopped at a café on the A74 just north of Carlisle, by special arrangement with the driver this group was accidentally left behind. As they chased after the coach on its way out of the car park, nearly a hundred fingers could be seen waving furiously in their direction.

That at least is how the story is told today, no doubt embellished somewhat by the passage of time but essentially true. Apparently it was a noisy journey—noisy enough to rival the coaches which every two years take tens of thousands of Scottish football supporters to the England match at Wembley. This coach of Militant-haters contained just as much venom as any contingent of the 'Tartan Army' of football fans and just as much singing. But, unlike most of their soccer predecessors, these Scotsmen were to return victorious.

Until the mid-1970s Militant had never really encountered any serious or concerted opposition in the Labour Party. The LPYS had been taken over in 1970 with hardly any argument; the granting of a place on the NEC to the LPYS in 1972, and the abolition of the famous Proscribed List a year later, almost gave official sanction to the tendency's activities. As the tendency grew more confident that it was secure in the party, *Militant* was sold more openly at party meetings. By the mid-1970s it seemed most unlikely that Militant could be toppled in the party's youth section. However, Militant's second major victory, the taking over of the Labour students body, NOLS, in January 1974, prompted an immediate reaction. This was matched by a growing feeling among many party officials that something had to be done about Militant, but a combination of bad organization, lack of willpower and political alliances ensured that Militant survived this opposition virtually unharmed.

The opposition to Militant in the Labour Party youth sections was symbolized by the icepick, the weapon used by a Stalinist agent to kill Trotsky in 1940—though the students on the coach had mistakenly used a mountaineering icepick. 'Operation Icepick', a serious attempt to out-manoeuvre Militant, was to make future Labour Party sectarianism look mild by comparison.

During the January 1974 NOLS Conference in

Manchester (at which Militant took control) several non-Militant delegates marched out of the conference hall after the platform had accepted the credentials of a number of Militant delegates which the non-Militant group believed to be false. The protesters gathered in the lounge on the eighteenth floor of the Owen's Park tower block and agreed to form a group specifically to oppose Militant. At first they could not think of a title, so initially their bank account went under the name of OIP—Operation Icepick. Later the group adopted the name Clause 4 after the famous section in the Labour Party constitution which calls for common ownership.

Clause 4 decided that it had to employ much the same kind of discipline and tactics as those used so successfully by Militant over the years. And in NOLS at least it was to be rewarded within two years. Clause 4 candidates won back NOLS in December 1975, and at the December 1976 Lancaster Conference—the destination of the Icepick Express—the battle between the two factions reached its peak. First a Clause 4 chairperson was elected by ninety-four votes to seventy-eight. Then Clause 4 candidates were elected to nearly all the other positions by precisely the same margin: ninety-four to seventy-eight.[1] Both sides at the conference had been almost perfectly disciplined; every delegate could be counted on to vote one way or the other. For once Militant had been beaten at its own game. As one prominent Clause 4 member put it later, 'We out-Militanted Militant.'

Like Militant, the Clause 4 organization officially centred on a journal, a bulletin called *Clause Four*, and the group was run by the journal's editorial board. Organizers were appointed to look after each region of the country and to co-ordinate LPYS and student work. There was also an annual Clause 4 conference. Unlike Militant, Clause 4 had no full-time staff—the members did not have sufficient commitment to cough up enough money for them—but Clause 4 did benefit from the work and resources of supporters who held sabbatical posts in student unions. Caucus meetings were arranged before every meeting of the NOLS National Committee; resolutions were sent out to Clause 4 members in Labour clubs and LPYS branches to be put forward for the national conferences of NOLS or the LPYS. At those conferences Clause 4 would hire a hotel for all its delegates and observers and would hold caucus meetings late into the evening to decide on tactics for the following day. By breakfast time 'whips' would have been issued to remind all Clause 4 delegates how to vote. But there was no 'democratic centralism': Clause 4 delegates were not obliged to toe the line: it was just a matter of political convenience.

Politically Clause 4 described itself as 'Tribunite'. Its outlook was broadly similar to that of the Tribune Group of MPs and the *Tribune* newspaper at that time—what would today be called 'soft left', roughly the position of Neil Kinnock. Clause 4 members sold copies of *Tribune* at Labour Party gatherings as if it were a rival paper to *Militant*, but they received little encouragement from either the *Tribune* newspaper or the parliamentary group. The then editor of *Tribune*, Dick Clements, did not wish to become involved in battles between different groups on the left of the party. Many former Clause 4 members feel today that had Clements and the leaders of the Tribune Group been more enthusiastic at that time, Clause 4 might have met with more success.

Clause 4 received great encouragement from Labour Party officials, though at that time they had to be careful not to be seen as partisan. The then National Youth Officer, Barrie Clarke, can admit today, now that Militant is officially outlawed, that he worked 'totally in league' with the Clause 4 organization. Clarke had succeeded Neil Vann as National Youth Officer in 1974 and served in this position for more than two years. He took on the job determined to do all he could to beat Militant. He kept in close touch with the

Clause 4 leadership and spent much of his time investigating Militant. The records of the Militant companies at Companies House in the City of London were scrutinized, and a photographer was posted outside Militant's offices to take pictures of all comings and goings. At every LPYS or NOLS conference Clarke would carefully examine the credentials of Militant delegates to see that they were in order and did not hesitate to disqualify any that were not: 'Much of my job as National Youth Officer was "disorganizing" as much as organizing. I was acting like a fire brigade, going round the country saying, "No, they can't do that."'[2]

The battle between the two sides was very bitter; there seemed to be no limit to the kinds of tactics that people would employ. Militant was becoming increasingly frustrated by its failure in NOLS: it began sending to its members lists of the universities to which it wanted them to apply, those where Militant votes were most needed. On one occasion in 1977 it was discovered that some of the NOLS delegates from Handsworth College were not actually members of the college. At one conference somebody even tried to electrocute Barrie Clarke. The wires to the Labour Party duplicator were deliberately connected up incorrectly. It was not Clarke who suffered, however, but his secretary when she came down early the next morning to print that day's agenda.

Clause 4 was to keep its hold on NOLS for the rest of the 1970s, but its record in the LPYS was disastrous. This was partly the result of a deliberate decision: Clarke believed that by concentrating on the student body Clause 4 could make reasonable progress and could perhaps show the Labour NEC what could be done, whereas the LPYS was regarded as beyond redemption. But its failure in the LPYS was partly also to do with the nature of Clause 4 itself. Because of its origins in NOLS, it was very much a student organization: university-orientated and middle-class. Many working-class people who sympathized with Clause 4's aims were put off by the atmosphere this created. The result was that it rested on its laurels in NOLS and ignored the LPYS almost completely, which meant that Clause 4 candidates at LPYS conferences got derisory results. Over the years Militant's grip on the LPYS has tightened, and the tendency has never been in any danger of losing control. Today Militant is so strong in the LPYS that it can not only guarantee to win all elections but even puts up second candidates just in case any winning nominees should be disqualified or should fall under the wheels of a bus and runners-up be required to take their places.[3]

The other problem with Clause 4 was that it was not politically positive. The group knew what it disliked more than what it liked. Though professing to be left-wing, in reality it was no more than an alliance of people who detested Militant, especially in the early days. It did produce some good work on policy matters and it published pamphlets, usually as a result of individual efforts, but Clause 4's time, energy and resources were spent largely in attacking Trotskyism rather than in proposing a coherent alternative. And the sectarianism was as marked as anything generated by Militant itself. Clause 4 produced badges and plastic pens with icepicks on them. At the end of one Christmas conference members performed a pantomime, dancing around the hall waving icepicks in the air. There was even a Clause 4 songbook.

Clause 4 took a far more serious approach to the National Union of Students (NUS) than Militant had done when it ran NOLS, and by the 1980s NOLS candidates were being elected to the NUS Executive. But the importance of Clause 4, and of its success in NOLS and the NUS, can easily be over-emphasized: in Britain student politics are of little importance to anyone but students and amount, on the whole, merely to practice in the ways of politicians.

For several Clause 4 leaders, however, that practice was invaluable in the careers they pursued later. Nigel Stanley, the

Clause 4 NOLS Chairman in 1978, became Organizing Secretary of the Labour Co-ordinating Committee and a leading member of the Rank and File Mobilizing Committee which in 1980 introduced two important changes to the party constitution: reselection of MPs, and the introduction of a wider franchise to elect the leadership.[4] Stanley used many of the skills he had developed in combating Militant to fight for these changes. (He is now political adviser to Neil Kinnock's right-hand man, Robin Cook.) Mike Gapes, NOLS Chairman in 1976, later became Labour Party Student Organizer and now works in the International Department. Gapes and several of his former colleagues stood as Labour candidates in the 1983 election and, perhaps significantly for the future, some were active in the campaign to get Neil Kinnock elected as leader.

In the meantime Militant has had no further success in NOLS, but nowadays organized opposition to the tendency comes from a wider 'democratic left' grouping. At the 1983 NOLS Conference Clause 4 had only eight delegates.

While plots against Militant were being hatched late at night over coffee in student digs, concern about Trotskyists was also growing at the highest levels of the Labour Party—in the office of the then National Agent, Reg (now Lord) Underhill. Underhill had long been an opponent of far-left elements in the party. As far back as the 1939 Conference, when he was a delegate from Leyton, he had spoken in a debate on the League of Youth and had referred to 'silly people talking of Trotsky, attacking the party and leaving the rest of the youth stone cold'.[5] After the war, in his position as Assistant to the National Agent and then as West Midlands Regional Organizer, Underhill had tried to tackle Communist infiltration in the Labour League of Youth. By the early 1960s, when he was Assistant National Agent, the problem was again Trotskyists, mainly from the Socialist Labour League.

Ever since Militant's takeover of the LPYS in 1970 Under-hill had been gathering evidence against the tendency. Most of it came from his team of regional organizers dotted around the country—a pretty right-wing group, many of whom had been appointed in the Gaitskellite days of the 1950s and early 1960s. Over the years several of Militant's internal docu-ments had been passed on to Underhill from the regional offices. He had discovered infiltration before, but what he read now about Militant came as a genuine shock. 'The first edition of "British Perspectives and Tasks" [Militant's internal document] I saw horrified me. Here was a group of members of the Labour Party setting out on paper how they would work inside the party.'[6]

In September 1975 Underhill got the NEC's consent to prepare a report on entrism based upon the documents he had received from regional organizers and on conversations with local party officials about Militant's activities. But Underhill's aim at that point was not to expel Militant from the party: 'I just wanted to bring it to the party's attention. At that time I thought we could handle it.'[7]

Underhill's report of November 1975 on 'Entryist Activi-ties' was a short, nine-page document.[8] One section of it covered other Trotskyist groups who had previously operated in the Labour Party, such as the Socialist Labour League (now the Workers' Revolutionary Party) and the International Socialists (now the Socialist Workers' Party). Another part dealt with the International Marxist Group, the body which in 1965 had taken over from Militant as the official British section of the Fourth International and which, Underhill reported, was now starting to mole its way into the Labour Party. But most of the report was devoted to Militant and contained extensive quotations from internal Militant documents, 'British Perspectives and Tasks 1974' and the pamphlet 'Entrism', a copy of which fell into Underhill's hands just before his report was presented.

The Underhill report gave an accurate picture of Militant's structure and strategy. It detailed the strength of the tendency, the extent of its organization and staff, its international links, the ways in which members were recruited and its long-term plans, which included establishing a group of about six Militant MPs. Yet the document made little impact on the NEC. On the day on which it came before the NEC's Organization Sub-Committee (known as the 'Org-Sub') very few members of the committee bothered to turn up. Eric Heffer successfully proposed that because of the low turnout the committee should let the report 'lie on the table'—in other words, they should do nothing. 'There have been Trotskyists in the Labour Party for thirty years,' Heffer remarked, with the benefit of personal experience (his own constituency, Liverpool Walton, had been a Trotskyist stronghold almost since the war). He argued that the 'threat' should be met with 'political arguments'. The motion was seconded by the Militant Young Socialist member, Nick Bradley, who said Militant was just like the *Tribune* newspaper and had no organization.[9] 'Reg, you've been conned,' he told Underhill.

When the Org-Sub's report came to the full Executive, the railwaymen's union member, Russell Tuck, and Shirley Williams tried to reverse the decision. But in spite of a long statement from Harold Wilson about the dangers of extremists on both sides of the party, the NEC accepted the Organization Sub-Committee's decision by sixteen votes to twelve.[10]

In 1975 the National Executive was dominated by the left, and the left–right split was more clear-cut than it is today: the Tribunites were united against the right, not divided between 'soft' and 'hard', as they have been recently. Many members of the Executive, such as Barbara Castle and, in particular, Michael Foot, thought they were seeing the start of another purge;[11] among those on the left Underhill had a long-standing reputation as a witch-hunter who had been involved in the discipline of the 1950s.

Some trade union NEC members knew very little about Militant beyond the Underhill report itself. When Nick Bradley claimed that Underhill's documents were forgeries, some Executive members may have been sufficiently out of touch to believe him.

The decision effectively to ignore Militant was yet another in a long series of embarrassments for Wilson caused by the Labour NEC. Underhill himself was extremely 'upset'. Others in his position would have had no qualms about leaking the report, but Underhill saw himself as a loyal servant of the party. He would never have dreamed of doing such a thing. As it turned out, others did it for him.

The Underhill report 'provided a lot of fuel for the press'.[12]. *The Times* published two whole columns of extracts,[13] and the report received wide coverage in every other paper. Some journalists had carried out their own investigations, notably Nora Beloff of the *Observer*, who wrote a long front-page lead article entitled '"Trot" Conspirators inside the Labour Party—Revolutionary Plot is Exposed', which for the first time told the story of Ted Grant and the RSL.[14] (Grant replied with a solicitor's letter denying any link with the RSL.)[15] But the NEC's refusal to publish the Underhill report only intensified the speculation and the press coverage. The general reaction was: why not publish the report? What was there to hide? The story was a source of considerable discomfiture for the party and seemed to confirm public feeling that extremists were taking over local constituency parties.

That impression had been stimulated partly by the publicity over Reg Prentice, who in July 1975 had been dropped as a candidate by his constituency party in Newham North-East. Within days the Prime Minister, Harold Wilson, reacted by condemning what he termed 'small and certainly not necessarily representative groups' and 'infiltration from outside the constituency, sometimes by change of residence'.[16] The Prentice affair was to drag on for almost two years.

The 1970s saw Reg Prentice make a rapid journey across the political spectrum which was unparalleled in recent political history. He began the decade by criticizing the first Wilson Government for 'falling short of our socialist standards';[17] in 1972 he came joint top of the Shadow Cabinet poll as a member of the Tribune Group slate; by the end of the 1970s he was a junior Minister in Mrs Thatcher's newly elected Government. At the time in question, 1975, Prentice was passing through the right-wing outskirts of the Labour Party. He had clearly lost touch with his local party activists. Towards the end of the 1975 EEC referendum campaign Prentice had praised the cross-party unity of the pro-Marketeers as a 'refreshing experience'.[18]. He spoke then of the need for a Government of National Unity (regarded as a codeword for 'coalition') and had earlier accused the unions of 'welshing' on the social contract. Such outbursts were not the wisest way to win the hearts of local party activists. Prentice's undoing was largely his own fault: he had managed to 'combine the politics of a Jenkins with the manners of a Skinner', commented the *New Statesman*.[19] But the Newham party's decision was secured only after the case had been dragged through the press and through the courts. Two Oxford graduates, financed by the right-wing National Association for Freedom, came to Prentice's aid; one of them, Julian Lewis, moved into the constituency especially to rally support for the MP. They ended up taking local officials and even the National Agent, Reg Underhill, to court on the grounds they had not followed the proper procedures. Prentice's case did a great deal to advance the cause of re-selection, especially after he joined the Conservatives.

Every move in the Prentice affair was covered extensively

by the media. Here, apparently, was a 'moderate' Cabinet Minister being ousted by extremists. The Newham North-East constituency party was presented as a typical inner-city local party, a decrepit organization in a safe seat, ripe for takeover by bed-sit infiltrators. The party had very few members. Local officials had never really bothered with recruitment, simply because at that point Labour was never in any danger of losing at election time.[20] Harold Wilson's outburst had fuelled the popular belief that large numbers of left-wing activists spent their lives deliberately moving from constituency to constituency causing trouble. In the end the most notable bed-sit infiltrators proved to be Paul McCormick and Julian Lewis, the two students who had come to Prentice's defence.

Certainly it was true that many members of the Newham General Management Committee had lived in the constituency for only a few months, but that can be said of most London constituencies. Young people tend to live in different places for short periods of time. Militant was strong in Newham North-East, but it did not have a majority: when a new candidate was eventually selected the Militant nominee, Nick Bradley, got just over one-third of the votes.[21] Prentice was quick to point his finger at Militant, and in an internal document Militant claimed to have acted as the 'catalyst' in the constituency.[22] A key figure was Andy Bevan, a leading Militant member and National Chairman of the LPYS who had moved to the constituency with his wife a few months before Prentice was dropped. Bevan helped to set up a LPYS branch and became Vice-Chairman of the party, but the fact was that many of Prentice's other critics were not Militant supporters. The man who was regarded as the leader of the anti-Prentice group, Tony Kelly, for instance, was not a Militant member, although he did call himself a revolutionary Marxist. Prentice's opponents included a wide range of left-wingers and people who thought that his politics were wrong and that he was not a good MP. Militant itself was delighted to take the blame (or glory) for getting rid of Prentice, especially when the MP later joined the Conservatives. Most important for our story, however, are not the facts of the Prentice affair or whether Militant played an important role in Newham but rather the impression these events gave that the Labour Party was being taken over by extremists.

Andy Bevan was at the centre of another major controversy over Militant which began a year later, in the autumn of 1976. This issue probably did more than anything else to intensify concern about Militant. After little more than two years as National Youth Officer, Barrie Clarke was somewhat relieved to be promoted to Political Education Officer. Around twenty people applied for the vacant post, but the final choice was between Terry Ashton, a young constituency agent, and Bevan, who was still Chairman of the LPYS. The selection panel consisted of three people: Bryan Stanley of the Post Office Engineering Union in the chair; Ron Hayward, the Labour Party's General Secretary; and Herbert Hickling of the General and Municipal Workers' Union. Bevan was impressive at the interview, coming across as able, charming and energetic. Ashton, regarded as the favourite for the job, had arrived late. Somehow he had been told to turn up at the wrong time and was hot and flustered. Hickling, a blunt trade unionist on the right of the party, was much struck by Bevan and, to everybody's surprise, said that there was no other choice. Ron Hayward, believing perhaps that a former poacher might make a good gamekeeper, seconded this. Ashton got the support of Stanley, but the job went to Bevan by two votes to one. No one was more surprised than Bevan himself, who had thought that for political reasons he did not stand a chance. Although Underhill had briefed the panel about Bevan's links with Militant, it seems that Bert Hickling did not really appreciate what Militant was. Bevan had got the job almost by accident. And since it was traditional for party appointments to be ratified automatically by the NEC, it now looked as though it was too late to reverse it.

Political considerations aside, Bevan probably deserved to be appointed. Even his critics conceded he had considerable ability; right-wing NEC member John Cartwright (now an SDP MP) said that Bevan was 'probably the most effective National Chairman of the Young Socialists there has been'.[23] Brought up in Swansea, Bevan was active in the National Union of School Students and later turned down a place at New College, Oxford, in favour of Bristol University because he thought Oxford 'petty-bourgeois'. As a student Bevan had pursued what could be described as a typical Trotskyist career, making rousing speeches in the students' union but never standing for positions which would involve a lot of bureaucratic work. In the LPYS he quickly rose to be National Chairman and was extremely popular. Like many leading Militant figures, Bevan gets on with people and always has time to stop and chat, even to political opponents.

The appointment caused uproar and was naturally seized on by the press. It did not take long for the tabloids to call Bevan 'Red Andy'.[24] The *Daily Telegraph* said that the Labour Party's appointment of a Trotskyist was the equivalent of the Conservatives employing a Nazi.[25] When the matter came before the full NEC in November the new leader Jim Callaghan managed to get the approval delayed because a number of Cabinet colleagues had not been able to turn up. At the December meeting Callaghan argued fervently against Bevan's appointment, and Hayward now seemed to be having second thoughts; but the NEC maintained tradition and accepted Bevan by fifteen votes to twelve. The meeting also rejected what it called 'a further descent into McCarthyism'.[26] It was nearly a straight left-right split. This time, though, the right was joined by Michael Foot, who had been alarmed by a speech of Bevan's a few days before, in which he had advocated the withdrawal of Britain's 'imperialist' troops from Ireland and had called the Irish Prime Minister a 'gangster' and the Northern Ireland peace campaigners 'bigots'.[27] Leading the supporters of Andy Bevan was Tony Benn, who opposed Callaghan publicly by publishing in the *Guardian* an article which Transport House had refused to circulate to the NEC.[28] Benn's defence of Bevan's appointment occupied a whole page, and it argued that Marxism was 'one of the many sources of inspiration within our movement'. Benn said that he knew Bevan personally: the two had worked closely in Benn's Bristol constituency in the 1974 election. Bevan had been effective in the local party: Benn said his speeches had impressed other party members, who had recognized in them 'the authentic voice of a political faith they have not heard advocated with such moral force since their own youth'.[29] The December 1976 NEC meeting was the first occasion on which Bevan was to find Benn a useful ally.

The Labour Party seems to have a remarkable ability to make its internal disputes drag on for ages. The row over Bevan was no exception. After the December NEC meeting the agents' union, the National Union of Labour Organizers, refused to work with him on the grounds that he was not a properly trained agent. When Bevan reported for work in January Hayward had to send him home on full pay. The agents did have a genuine grievance: they were earning £3,000 a year on average, while Bevan would be getting £4,000 and had no previous experience as an agent. But the dispute was mainly political and was resolved only when the NEC agreed that an inquiry should now examine the Underhill documents. Bevan's position was somewhat reduced in importance when the NEC agreed to give his student tasks to a new Student Organizer.

Bevan's appointment had again stimulated wide press

coverage of Militant. *The Times* ran a long series on the tendency the week before the December meeting.[30] These articles 'revealed' that twelve MPs felt threatened by Militant. Apart from Prentice, two other right-wing MPs, Neville Sandelson in Hayes and Harlington and Frank Tomney in Hammersmith North, were both at war with their parties. There was even speculation that Jim Callaghan was in danger in Cardiff South-East. This press attention, fuelled by right-wingers such as Sandelson, had played an important part in forcing the Labour Party to hold its inquiry.

The inquiry team consisted of two union members, John Chalmers and Tom Bradley, together with two MPs, Eric Heffer and Michael Foot, and General Secretary Ron Hayward. Eric Heffer was initially against any action. Michael Foot, though he did not like the idea of a 'party within a party', did not care for witch-hunts either. When the inquiry team reported four months later, in May 1977, it had managed to hammer out a typical Labour Party compromise, avoiding disciplinary action but accepting that Militant was in breach of the rules. The report's recommendations, drawn up by Eric Heffer, were largely cosmetic. Local parties were urged to recruit new members and to make meetings more interesting. The report said that the Young Socialists should not be 'an organization with only limited membership and a narrow appeal' and called on local parties to 'intensify the development of political education' and to hold discussions, lectures and day schools to explain the Labour Party's belief in democratic socialism. But the report urged tolerance, arguing that 'Trotskyist views cannot be beaten by disciplinary action.'[31]

Militant had escaped again. Nothing came of the Heffer recommendations. The LPYS remained small in numbers and lacking in appeal; no local party is known to have carried out the education suggested. For the next two years the Militant issue was dormant. It was becoming increasingly difficult to rock the boat when Labour's precarious position in Parliament made an election possible at any moment. Meanwhile Militant took advantage of the greater access it had to the Labour headquarters. For example, young people who wrote in to join the party were frequently visited by members of Militant before they had been contacted by local Labour officials.

By the late 1970s Militant had been brought out into the open, but it had little to fear while the NEC was held by the left. Most left-wingers on the NEC were firmly opposed to witch-hunts, remembering well the atmosphere in the Labour Party in the 1950s and the time when Bevan had almost been expelled from the party. At the same time the left wanted Militant's support against the right in impending internal battles, such as those over party democracy. (That support was not always forthcoming: in 1977 Militant wrecked an early attempt to introduce mandatory reselection by proposing its own more radical motion to Conference.) Some NEC members felt that an attack on Militant was also an attack on the Young Socialists, who were traditionally given extra leeway to allow for their youthful excesses. 'Don't you think we're being a bit hard on the youth?' the Youth Committee chairman, Frank Allaun, used to say whenever Barrie Clarke produced another controversial report. Joan Maynard frequently complained about people attacking 'the lads and lasses'.[32] It was only in later years that many of Militant's defenders on the left, in private at least, were to become more critical of the tendency.

6

The Organization

Travel by train from Liverpool Street Station in London to Cambridge, and after about two and a half miles you pass through a small station in Hackney called London Fields. To the west of the railway at this point is the park from which the station takes its name; on the other side, running parallel to the line, is a street called Mentmore Terrace. On one side of the street, under the railway arches, are small workshops; while the other side of Mentmore Terrace has a row of rather run-down Victorian houses and, at No. 1, a building on its own, which was once a cardboard box factory.

This is the Centre, the headquarters of Militant since 1976. It is one of three buildings that the tendency uses, all within a few hundred yards of each other, here on the borders of Hackney and Bethnal Green in the East End of London, the land of the rag trade and second-hand car dealers. From outside the Centre does not look much: passers-by might easily assume that the place is deserted. The grilles over the windows are the only clue to the revolutionary activity within. The quiet exterior is misleading: at all hours of the day people are working inside. Well over thirty full-timers are employed here and many more regular volunteers. The building is not just an editorial office: it houses the tendency's three main printing presses, and there is a small shop selling books and pamphlets. But, above all, it is the heart of Militant's extensive political organization.

The only room in the building normally open to outsiders is the bookshop, just inside the front door: it is in here that visiting journalists have to conduct their interviews, against a suitable backdrop of the works of Marx, Engels, Lenin, Trotsky, Grant and Taaffe. The rest of the building is barred to 'non-comrades' on grounds of 'security': inquiring journalists are politely told of the times when the building has been attacked by fascists. Very few outsiders have ever been inside.

No. 375 Cambridge Heath Road, half a mile away, was bought by the tendency in 1970 and was the main office before Mentmore Terrace. It is a three-storey terraced building on the High Street, a few hundred yards north of Bethnal Green Underground station. The outside is painted dark red, and these premises too look empty—the only sign that anybody has been inside in the last ten years is a brand-new doorbell. At one time the property belonged to the local Boy Scouts; now, appropriately, it is used as a base for Militant's Youth Bureau, which co-ordinates the tendency's work in the LPYS. It also houses the International Bureau.

Cambridge Heath Road runs north. When it passes into the Borough of Hackney, its name changes to Mare Street. At 300 Mare Street, just past Hackney Town Hall and on the other side of the road, is the third Militant London office, above a former branch of Barclay's Bank. The bank has moved to new premises next door, and the lease on No. 300 is now owned by Hackney Council, which uses the ground floor as a housing office and rents the top floor to Militant. This office, which houses a small computer, is where Clare Doyle looks after the extensive Militant finances, which we shall be looking at in detail in the next chapter.

In addition to these properties, Militant also has regional offices in several other cities, including Liverpool, Newcastle and Birmingham. In other towns—Brighton and Bristol, for instance—the tendency has rooms in members' houses. These are used as regional bookshops and meeting places and many have duplicating machines for local printing work.

At the very top of the Militant hierarchy is the Executive Committee (referred to publicly as the Editorial Board) which, Militant asserts, consists of five people: Peter Taaffe, the editor of *Militant*; Ted Grant, the political editor; Lynn Walsh, the assistant editor; Clare Doyle, the business manager; and Keith Dickinson, in charge of administration and security. These were the five who were expelled from the Labour Party in February 1983. Three of them, Taaffe, Grant and Dickinson, have been at the centre of Militant since the very beginning of its newspaper in 1964. Walsh and Doyle are both from the group once based at Sussex University and joined the organization in the mid-1960s but did not become key figures until later.

Peter Taaffe was born into a family of six children in Birkenhead during the war. His father, a sheet-metal worker, died when he was a child, and the family lived in what Taaffe describes as 'atrocious housing':[1] he still has a scar on the bridge of his nose which is a legacy from the time when the ceiling fell down on him while he was asleep in bed. Taaffe mixes well. He gets on with working people and understands them; he will have a drink with the lads, talk about television or football and his favourite team, Everton. At lunchtime you will often find him playing soccer on London Fields with other Militant staff (Taaffe is always allowed to pick the best side). He is married with two teenage daughters. His wife Linda sometimes writes for *Militant*, usually on women's issues, and is active in the Labour Party in Islington. Before his expulsion Taaffe himself had not been seen at his local ward party for several years.

The eccentric Ted Grant is a more private character than Taaffe, and he enjoys the air of mystery that surrounds him. His whole life has been devoted to revolutionary politics. He has few hobbies; one of them is table tennis, at which he always beats Taaffe, much to the editor's annoyance. Beethoven and Bach are another diversion. Grant very rarely drinks and is obsessed with keeping fit and healthy, eating health foods and doing exercises every morning. His only known vices are jelly-babies and gobstoppers. Militant's other leaders are resigned to the fact that even though Grant is now over 70, he will be around for the next twenty years. He often teases Taaffe that he will outlive him. Certainly Grant appears to be ten years younger than his real age. Even so, Militant colleagues sometimes refer to Grant as the 'Old Man' (the nickname given to Trotsky himself in the 1930s). On public occasions he is often seen in smart, expensive clothes, but he never wears them well: it is said in Militant that Grant is paid so badly by the organization that his clothes have been passed on to him by his sister's husband, a wealthy businessman in France. Grant did not become a full-timer with Militant until 1969; Taaffe and Dickinson were employed by the tendency before him. Until then he carried on working as a night-time telephone operator. Grant's office at the Centre contains hundreds of books by and about Marx, Lenin, Engels, Trotsky and Plekhanov. The walls are piled high with back issues of the *Banker*, the *Economist*, *Investors Chronicle* and the *Financial Times*: he even has copies of the *FT* going back to the 1930s. One can always recognize articles written by Grant: they are sprinkled with quotations from these journals, using 'capitalist' quotations against capitalism.

The relationship between Taaffe and Grant is an interesting one. Officially Taaffe is editor of *Militant*; in reality he does little work on the paper. His real job is General Secretary. Nominally he occupies a position superior to Grant's, but it was Grant who helped to appoint Taaffe in the first place, and Grant has assumed the role of keeping Militant's ideology 'pure'. Broadly speaking, Taaffe is responsible for organization and Grant for political and economic analysis. As we have seen, Grant played a similar role with Jock Haston in the RCP in the 1940s and, less successfully, with Jimmy Deane in the RSL in the 1950s. In the unlikely event that Militant ever came to power, one could speculate that Grant would be President (once the monarchy had been abolished) and Taaffe would continue as General Secretary of the party and probably Prime Minister as well. Grant is the theoretician; Taaffe masterminds the strategy, putting the theories into practice. This is only a rough guide to their comparative functions: the two men would have difficulty explaining their relationship themselves. Taaffe does have an important policy role too, and he writes a great deal. Their respective roles also seem to be changing: with time Taaffe has gradually been taking on even more responsibility and power. Grant appears to be on the decline.

Peter Taaffe often finds Grant difficult to cope with in public. On one occasion when Militant's leaders met the Labour Party NEC, the General Secretary Jim Mortimer complained that certain Militant supporters had been causing trouble. 'Then give us the names,' shot back Grant, 'and we'll discipline them.'[2] Peter Taaffe was clearly embarrassed by his colleague's indiscretion. Once, during a television interview, he took out his handkerchief and energetically wiped his nose. Grant is famous throughout the Labour movement for his mannerisms and violent hand movements while speaking: these are frequently imitated by Militant's younger members, sometimes in admiration but often in jest.

The assistant editor of *Militant*, Lynn Walsh, is one of the younger generation of Militant leaders bred politically at Sussex University in the mid-1960s. After university he lectured in a college of technology and then became a Militant full-timer. During the early 1970s he became a specialist on Spain and Portugal, spending a lot of time in both countries, where Militant had high expectations after the fall of the two dictatorships. Walsh is obviously middle-class and does not feel the need to conceal it by adopting a Liverpool or East End accent, as do some of his more self-conscious middle-class colleagues. He avoids many of the stock phrases and clichés and, presumably because of his more natural manner, often chairs Militant press conferences. In practice it is Walsh, not Taaffe, who edits the paper. He writes many of the editorials; Taaffe casts an eye over them later.

The only woman in the Militant leadership, Clare Doyle, is publicly the organization's business manager and internally treasurer of the tendency. Like Walsh, she joined the Labour Party in Brighton in 1964. The daughter of a vicar from Sussex, she was once married to another prominent Militant character, Peter Doyle, Chairman of the LPYS in the early 1970s and the first LPYS representative on the NEC before it was discovered he was too old. They met through Militant when Clare was working on Tyneside as a nursery-school teacher. She hit the national headlines during the Toxteth riots in 1981, when she went to Liverpool to distribute leaflets and to explain to the Liverpool comrades what could be learned from Brixton, where she lives.

Keith Dickinson is responsible for Militant administration and for running the offices. He is also in charge of security, which means not only protecting Militant's properties but also vetting all Militant documents, internal and public, for slips which might give something away. Nicknamed 'the Nag', Dickinson was for eight years (until 1983) caretaker of the committee rooms of the Hammersmith Labour Party and lived in a flat above them. Of the five expelled in 1983 Dickinson is probably the most active in the Labour Party: he has served on the Hammersmith party's General Committee for several years and has stood unsuccessfully in several council elections. He first joined the Labour Party in Liverpool Walton in 1957 and in 1960 spoke in the famous Conference debate on defence in which Hugh Gaitskell made his 'Fight, fight and fight again' speech. One of the founders of the *Militant* newspaper, he had previously been on the editorial boards of *Rally* and *Socialist Fight* as well as business manager of *Young Guard*, which was eventually taken over by the Cliff group (later the Socialist Workers' Party). Dickinson is a shy person—you will more often see him sitting at the back of the hall than on the platform at the front—but he is very popular within the tendency.

These five ostensibly form Militant's Editorial Board. In reality, though, the Executive usually contains about ten people. The five well-known names were simply listed for public consumption when the Labour Party was about to expel people. Who else is on the Executive, then? It is fairly safe to assume that it includes the heads of Militant's three most important bureaux (departments)—International (Roger Silverman), Youth (Tony Saunois) and Industrial (Brian Ingham). These three have frequently been billed at public meetings with the same prominence as the self-styled 'Militant Five' and, significantly, Ingham and Silverman were named in reply to a questionnaire from the Labour Party in 1980. Others who appear to be quite important, and who are therefore likely to be on the Executive, are John Pickard, one of *Militant*'s leading journalists, and Alan Woods, who in 1983 returned from Spain to edit Militant's theoretical journal, *Militant International Review*.

Militant's organization is based on the principles of a Marxist–Leninist revolutionary party. Its style of administration is that of most democratic centralist parties—the party system devised by Lenin for the Bolsheviks in Russia, which later came to be adopted by all Communist parties.

The Militant Executive Committee has a function similar to that of the Politburo in most Communist parties. Every Friday it meets to make the day-to-day decisions for the tendency. The larger Central Committee (until 1974 called the National Committee) consists of about forty-five people and includes representatives from each of the regions and the tendency's bureaux. It meets every two or three months at the Centre to sort out broader, longer-term policy and organizational matters. Apart from the elected members, other regular attenders at Central Committee meetings are some of the full-timers and Militant members on the LPYS National Committee. At one time Militant went even further in the tradition of democratic centralist parties and had 'alternate members' of its Central Committee; these were expected to attend the Committee's meetings and could speak but were allowed to vote only if any full members were absent. A few years ago alternate membership of the Committee was abolished, though, and the Committee itself was enlarged.

At the next level down in the hierarchy, below the Central Committee, are the full-timers. 'Full-timer' is a political rank in Militant rather than an indication that one is a paid employee. Full-timers do not apply for the position; they are simply appointed by the Executive Committee, and once a Militant member gets the call he or she is expected to give up existing employment. In most cases full-timers go through a training period beforehand, but even after this they may not necessarily be paid by the organization: many full-timers claim state benefits, especially those who were unemployed before working for Militant. Sometimes these dole payments will be topped up by extra money from Militant—for instance, in the form of over-generous expenses. Other full-timers are so badly paid that they have to live off the earnings of their spouses, who will nearly always be members of the tendency. At the time of writing Militant has over 130 people in the 'full-timer' position, more than twice as many as it has acknowledged publicly for the past three years (sixty-four). This compares well with established political parties. The Labour Party has about 200 full-time staff in all, adding together those in London, its regional offices and the constituencies. The Social Democrats now have around thirty (following redundancies the SDP had to make after the 1983 election) and the Liberals have about fifty employees in total. The former Liberal Party Secretary-General, Hugh Jones, often complained of having fewer staff than Militant. By comparison with simple Labour Party pressure groups Militant is even better off. Labour Solidarity has just two full-time staff, one paid and one voluntary; the Fabian Society has six; and the *Tribune* newspaper employs the equivalent of seven full-timers. Even the *New Statesman*, with a slightly larger circulation than *Militant*, employs only about two dozen people. Indeed, if one leaves aside trade unions, Militant has far more full-time workers than all the dozens of other Labour Party pressure groups and news-papers put together.

About half the full-timers work in Militant's three offices in London: as journalists on the paper, as print workers or in Militant's bureaux: Political, Finance, Industrial, Youth, Black and Asian, Student and International. The rest of the full-timers are scattered around the country. Outside London the more senior of these have overall responsibility for a region; others concentrate on regional youth or industrial work, or work in a particular district within the region.

Below the full-timers are the cadres—*la crème de la crème* of the ordinary members—those perfectly 'steeled' in the ideas of the tendency, as Peter Taaffe would put it, and those who have been around a long time and are not seen as a security risk. Originally, since the RSL saw itself as a cadre organiz-ation, all members were considered to be cadres. This meant they had both a sound political education in the tendency's ideas and political experience. But in recent times, as mem-bership has expanded, the term 'cadre' within the tendency has come to refer to between 300 and 500 leading and long-serving members. The aim is that in time every member will become a cadre. In turn cadres are encouraged to achieve sufficiently high standards to enable them to be selected as full-timers.

Ever since the beginning of the RSL there has been an annual conference or 'congress', as it was called in the very early days. These are now held in the autumn, and the venue since 1979 has always been Bridlington. The gathering is held with the utmost secrecy: security is impressive. Only members bearing special tickets ('V' for visitor and 'D' for delegate) are allowed in. Administrative reports are individually marked and numbered before being handed out and have to be returned at the end of each session. On one occasion cleaners were not even permitted to replace the towels in the lavatories, and the conference hall bar staff were not allowed to watch what was going on in spite of protestations that they were sympathetic. In 1980 several journalists tried to wheedle their way in, and one reporter was even found hiding in the lavatories. No journalist has ever succeeded in seeing what goes on, but the publicity given to the secret events has done Militant a lot of harm. In 1982, at the height of the Labour Party campaign against Militant, at the last minute it was thought best to cancel that year's conference. To placate the Labour NEC the tendency said that in future it would open the occasion to outsiders, but after the expulsion of the Militant Editorial Board this offer was withdrawn, and Militant returned to Bridlington in November 1983. Publicly the conference is always referred to as an annual *Militant* sellers' rally, for people who sell the paper regularly. In reality it is a full-scale party conference.

Each Militant branch sends delegates, one for every five members, but other members are encouraged to go too. (When the membership was small all members were strongly urged to attend.) The conference sessions are chaired by members of the Central Committee in rotation. Most of the two or three days is taken up with discussion of the latest copies of 'British Perspectives and Tasks' and 'World

Perspectives', the secret discussion documents written collectively by the Militant leadership every year. Before being presented to the conference, the 'Perspectives' will have been approved by the Executive and Central Committee and sent out to members in advance. All the conference is expected to do is to debate the documents and pass them unanimously. It always does. Amendments are rare.

The rest of the conference time is taken up with administrative matters. The General Secretary and the treasurer of the Militant organization, Peter Taaffe and Clare Doyle, give reports on organization and finance. There will also be accounts of the tendency's progress in other areas from the head of each bureau: Youth, International, Industrial and so on. At the end of the assembly comes a rallying speech from Ted Grant, which serves just the same purpose as the leader's speech at the end of a Conservative Conference. Then all the delegates return to their branches to give reports on the conference to the ordinary members and to outline the 'perspectives and tasks' for the year ahead.

Every year the conference also has the task of re-electing the Central Committee. In the true traditions of democratic centralism it usually does just that. As in most Marxist–Leninist parties, the outgoing Committee will propose to the conference their recommendations for the new Central Committee. Delegates can only pass or reject the list of names en bloc. They can propose other candidates for election, but only by putting forward an amendment to the official list, which also means proposing who should be replaced. Not surprisingly, challenges to the official list rarely occur, which explains the remarkable continuity of the Militant leadership over the years.

This is not to say that there are never any disagreements at Militant conferences. The 1973 gathering at Sheffield University saw a serious division when one group of fifteen members proposed a long alternative 'Perspectives' document calling for more involvement in single-issue campaigns and co-operation with other left-wing pressure groups. The dissidents were allowed to address the conference, and their document was circulated in advance by the Central Committee; but with support from only one branch, Nottingham, these 'petty-bourgeois' rebels were defeated overwhelmingly. Nevertheless the Militant leadership was seriously worried by the challenge and tried to conciliate the dissidents, in vain. After the defeat they left and joined the IMG.

The subject of devolution caused another serious split two years later. The Militant leadership wanted to change the tendency's position from anti- to pro-devolution. Most of the Scottish delegates to the conference, led by an alternate Central Committee member, Alex Wood, argued vehemently against this change of policy. The leadership won the battle, and Wood eventually left the tendency.

Since about 1978 the important decisions of the tendency have been hammered out in a new body, the National Council, which meets just once a year, a few months before the conference itself. This body comprises all the most trusted cadres—full-timers and delegates from each region and district, and it effectively decides beforehand what the conference will be asked to rubber-stamp.

Geographically the Militant organization is divided into regions, districts and branches. There are twelve regions in all: London, Southern, West Midlands, East Midlands, Eastern, South-West, Yorkshire and Humberside, Manchester and Lancashire, Merseyside, Northern, Wales, and Scotland. Though the names are broadly similar to those of the Labour Party regions, the boundaries have deliberately been drawn differently, perhaps to cause confusion to Labour officials. Within each region are several districts, each of which generally covers a conurbation or county. In turn each district is made up of a number of branches. The branch is the lowest organizational unit: it may cover a small town or part of a city, often the same area as a single parliamentary constituency. But it should be stressed that the system of districts and branches is only the ideal model. In some parts of the country, particularly in rural areas, Militant may not be strong enough to sustain branches or even districts, and in such cases the region forms the basic administrative unit. As the Militant organization has expanded, more and more districts and branches have been established: as soon as any one unit is big enough—more than about a dozen people—it will be split into two.

Each region, district and branch is administered by a committee, often referred to in public as a regional, district or local 'editorial board'. Nominally these committees are elected by all the members in the area they cover; in reality they are self-perpetuating groups nominated by themselves, just as the Central Committee is.

Branches meet weekly and are the ordinary members' main contact with the Militant organization. But even where branches are strong the regions and districts remain important levels in the Militant structure: the higher levels are given targets for new members and paper sales, and they look after Militant's financial contributions. In addition, all communications from the Centre come down to the branches via the regional and district full-timers. As well as weekly branch meetings, members will go to district 'aggregate' meetings—attended by all the members in the district—at least once a quarter. There is also an aggregate meeting for each region at least once a year. Then there are regular weekend 'cadre schools', organized by districts and regions, whose aim is to educate members in Marxist theory and to train them in political skills such as public speaking and selling papers.

Apart from its hierarchical structure covering the country, Militant organizes a number of caucuses for its work in particular trade unions and now has groups operating in nearly twenty different unions. Union work is becoming an increasingly important area for Militant because of the attention the tendency has received within the Labour Party. There is also a Black and Asian Militant caucus and a women's group. In addition Militant organizes a number of front organizations, which to outsiders have no obvious connection with the tendency. Among these are PNP Youth, a British youth section of the Jamaican National Party, which has tried, fairly unsuccessfully, to recruit young West Indians and even Asians to the tendency.

Apart from its newspaper, Militant produces a wide range of other publications, some public and some strictly internal. Among the former is the quarterly *Militant International Review*, a theoretical magazine which was started in 1969. Alan Woods recently took over as editor—a sign that he may assume part of Ted Grant's theoretical role in the future. There are also sporadic Militant publications for distribution in certain unions, such as *Militant Teacher*, *Militant Miner*, *NALGO Militant* and *Beacon*, the Militant journal for the electricians' union. On top of that are regular pamphlets and books on a wide range of subjects, from Marxist theory and ideological issues to the situation in particular countries and even CIA infiltration of the Labour Party.

Internal documents divide into two types: 'Perspectives', which are annual discussion documents, and 'Bulletins', which deal mainly with organizational matters and short-term strategy. 'British Perspectives and Tasks' is the main 'Perspectives' document, produced every year before the conference. (As there was no conference in 1982, it was not published.) It sets out the tendency's latest analysis of political and economic affairs in Britain and charts the progress and plans of Militant itself. 'World Perspectives', once called 'International Perspectives', does a similar job on the international scene and outlines Militant's plans for world revolution.

The main bulletin documents go out every quarter to all

branches. These include the 'Industrial Bulletin', the 'Student Bulletin', the 'Youth Bulletin' and the 'International Bulletin'. Finally Militant occasionally publishes one-off internal publications such as the famous reprinted pamphlet 'Entrism'.

All the secret documents are carefully written so as not to give away any details about who publishes or prints them. Militant is never referred to by name, only by phrases such as 'our tendency'. Once or twice, though, the man in charge of security, Keith Dickinson, has slipped up. The 1973 edition of 'Entrism', for instance, accidentally carried the Cambridge Heath Press imprint.[3] Articles are signed with pseudonyms (Peter Harris is Peter Taaffe) or with reversed initials (so TP is Peter Taaffe, GE Ted Grant, WP Pat Wall, DC Clare Doyle and so on), but often, especially on political matters, it is difficult to see the need for a secret internal document anyway. Sometimes there is little difference between what is published internally and what is distributed in public. 'British Perspectives 1981', for instance, is the same, almost word for word, as a pamphlet by Ted Grant entitled 'Britain in Crisis'. The only difference was that the private version had paragraph numbers, while the public one did not, and an unfavourable reference to Michael Foot was deleted from the public edition.

It is in these internal documents that one can find details of Militant's extensive international links. The 'CWI Bulletin No. 1', dated July 1974, reported on the founding of the Committee for the Workers' International (CWI) on 21 April 1974. The CWI saw a future Workers' International as the Militant successor to the Fourth International and the previous three internationals, joining together socialist contacts from other countries to further the cause of world revolution:

Forty-six comrades from twelve countries participated in the Founding Conference. This represented a great leap forward for our tendency. Nevertheless, there were still only four established national sections, in Britain, Ireland, Sweden and Germany. Other comrades attended as individual sympathizers. But as we go to press, organizations are being established in Spain, Portugal and Belgium. We are also in discussion with groups that are close to our ideas in Sri Lanka, Greece and Austria, and we are confident that these comrades will join us. Soon we will have more than doubled the number of national sections.[4]

The Committee for the Workers' International is very much a Militant-dominated body. During its period in the Fourth International, from 1956 to 1965, the RSL had never been a very enthusiastic member, enjoying the status but not the commitments that membership entailed. In 1965 Militant was expelled, and the British franchise was given to the IMG. But since 1974 the RSL has had its own international organization, led from Britain. Details of Militant's international links are difficult to find. Ordinary members of the Militant tendency are not well-informed about them, and certain contacts are kept highly secret. Militant groups operating abroad have met with less tolerance from socialist and social democratic parties than in Britain, and in certain Third World countries they fear strong action from Governments, which may mean imprisonment or worse.

But the *Militant* newspaper itself gave the game away only a few days after the CWI was founded. In the May Day 1974 edition of *Militant* were advertisements for foreign newspapers: *Offensiv*, the 'Marxist paper within the Swedish Labour movement'; *Voran*, the 'German Marxist paper'; and *Militant Irish Monthly*.[5] Together with *Militant* these three papers correspond exactly to the four sections of the CWI mentioned in the internal 'CWI Bulletin' quoted above. Later editions of *Militant* contained advertisements for other sister papers: *Vonk* (Belgium), *Xekinima* (Greece), *Voorwarts* (the Netherlands) and *Nuevo Claridad* (Spain). All these papers were available from Mentmore Terrace. Inspecting these journals, one finds constant references to the others; articles from one paper are often reprinted in sister papers, and most of them borrow *Militant* photos and cartoons.

But by comparison with Militant most of these groups are inconsequential: few have more than a few dozen members. Their journals are published sporadically, and Militant is as strong as all of them put together. Nor have any of these foreign 'Militant tendencies' had much success in the parties they have entered. The *Xekinima* group was expelled from the Greek socialist party, PASOK, in 1976 and the *Nuevo Claridad* group from the Spanish socialist party in the late 1970s. The Swedish Social Democrats have twice expelled members of the *Offensiv* tendency, and the *Voran* group in Germany has been thrown out of the German SPD.

At first Militant established most of its foreign groups in parties belonging to the Socialist International. Every year the LPYS is invited to send 'fraternal delegates' to the conferences of youth sections of parties in the Socialist International, and since taking over the LPYS Militant has managed to ensure that its own people are always appointed as the delegates. Their top priority when abroad is to discover sympathetic 'elements' and 'good material'. In this way most European parties in the Socialist International have had Militant groups inside them at one time or another. At the 1981 conference of the International Union of Socialist Youth in Austria—the youth section of the Socialist International—there was even a joint meeting between Militant and the *Voran* and *Offensiv* groups, and £380 raised in a collection was divided between the three.[6]

Militant's Irish section, centred on the paper *Militant Irish Monthly*, was started in 1972 and has sixteen members of staff operating from offices in Dublin and Belfast. In the Irish Republic Militant has now taken control of the Irish Labour

Party's youth section. This prompted an inquiry into its activities, and in January 1984 its Dublin office was raided by armed police officers. In Northern Ireland, Militant, under the name of the Labour and Trade Union Group, ran a candidate, Muriel Tang, in East Belfast in June 1983. Although she got only 584 votes (1.5 per cent), that was more than the Social Democratic and Labour Party received.

Militant's biggest foreign section is in Sri Lanka, one of the few countries ever to have had a mass Trotskyist party. The Lanka Sama Samaja Party, one of the coalition partners in the former Bandaranaike Government, split in the mid-1970s, and Militant supporters took over what remained and renamed it the Nava Sama Samaji Party (NSSP). On several occasions Ted Grant has visited Sri Lanka, as has Pat Wall; on the last occasion when Grant went there, in 1981, President Jayawardene's Government sent him home. Militant supporters have also controlled one of the two Sri Lankan trade unions, and when they tried to organize a general strike a few years ago several of them were thrown into jail. The Militant-controlled NSSP, with only about 600 members, is now very weak and the NSSP was one of the parties banned by the Government after the riots of 1983. *Militant* gave the troubles extensive coverage, and it was David Nellist, one of the two newly elected Militant MPs, who first raised the issue of the Sri Lanka troubles in the Commons.

In Pakistan the Militant group operates in great secrecy within the opposition Pakistan People's Party of the late President Bhutto and distributes a magazine called the *Struggle*. In South Africa a group calling itself the Marxist Workers' Tendency operates openly within the African National Congress, publishing a magazine *Inqaba Ya Basebenzi* ('Workers' Fortress'), which is printed at Mentmore Terrace. Militant also has groups of sympathizers in several other countries, including Cyprus, France, Italy, India and Jamaica. Since 1973 this work has been co-ordinated in the

International Bureau in London by Roger Silverman, who is now assisted by Bob Labi. But the CWI has made little progress outside Britain. Foreign socialist parties have shown far less tolerance than the British Labour Party, and have moved quickly to expel these groups. In most cases they are more centralized and have national membership lists, which makes disciplinary action much easier. The CWI still remains very much dominated by the British section, Militant, which set it up; and apart from the Sri Lankan and Irish groups, Militant is the only section with any significant strength. It seems that it will be some time before the Workers' International itself can be established.

This, then, is the Militant organization. It is the organization of a political party—and one operating secretly within the Labour Party—that practises entrism. It is this extensive organization, rather than political differences, which has provided the main argument for the recent action against Militant. In that debate the party establishment has turned to its own rule book to uphold its case. Clause II, Section 3, of the Labour Party constitution states:

> Political organizations not affiliated to or associated under a National Agreement with the Party on 1 January 1946, having their own Programme, Principles and Policy for distinctive and separate propaganda, or possessing Branches in the Constituencies or engaged in the promotion of Parliamentary or Local Government Candidates or owing allegiance to any political organization situated abroad, shall be ineligible for affiliation to the Party.[7]

That Militant is in breach of this part of the Labour Party constitution must be beyond doubt. It does have its 'own Programme, Principles and Policy for distinctive and separate

113

propaganda'. It does possess 'Branches in the Constituencies'. It does owe allegiance to a 'political organization situated abroad' (though the CWI's headquarters are actually at the Militant offices in London). On three points of Section 3 Militant is guilty. Only on the fourth count (promoting 'Parliamentary or Local Government Candidates') is Militant not breaching the constitution. Nevertheless, when five Militant supporters stood as Labour candidates in the 1983 election they stood on a Militant programme rather than on Labour's manifesto, and Militant treated them almost as if they were standing for its organization, not for Labour.

If Militant is breaking the Labour Party's rules, so, strictly speaking, are many other Labour Party pressure groups. Labour Solidarity, the Labour Co-ordinating Committee and the Campaign for Labour Party Democracy, to name only three of the most prominent groups, all have their own distinctive propaganda and policies. The Labour Co-ordinating Committee and several other groups have branches in the constituencies. Other bodies, such as Labour Friends of Israel and the Labour Committee for Europe, clearly have allegiance to 'political organizations situated abroad'; furthermore, they openly receive funds from abroad. The Labour Party constitution is so strict that dozens of pressure groups within the party ranks are in breach of it; but it has always been a tradition within the party to take the constitution with a pinch of salt, and Clause II, Section 3, has always been taken by all pressure groups, on the left and on the right, with a particularly large pinch. In just the same way many on the right have long ignored the famous Clause IV, Part 4, which calls for common ownership. Dislike of Militant has grown not simply because its organization has been in breach of the Labour Party's constitution—that is a widespread offence—but because it has breached the constitution so blatantly and, perhaps more important, so effectively.

114

7

Militant's Money

The financial year 1976–7 was a disaster in the eyes of Her Majesty's Treasury. The pound hit an all-time low against the dollar; twice the Chancellor had to announce cuts in public expenditure, on the second occasion after humiliating negotiations with the International Monetary Fund. The Public Sector Borrowing Requirement, the difference between government income and expenditure, was at its highest level ever. And the Labour Chancellor, Denis Healey, was not getting much help from British industry. That year thirteen of Britain's top twenty firms, including BP, Esso, Dunlop and Ford, managed to avoid paying any 'mainstream' Corporation Tax.[1] But if Healey received little support from the commanding heights of the economy, the Exchequer was at least benefiting from the efforts of one tiny company in Hackney, which was less than three years old but had great ambitions for international expansion. From No. 1 Mentmore Terrace, London E8, came a cheque for £546, the Corporation Tax payment on the profits of WIR Publications Limited, one of the two companies owned by Militant.[2]

For a left-wing organization to do well enough to pay tax on its profits, as WIR Publications has frequently done, is unusual. But then Militant has had an unusual financial history. Ever since the first issue of its newspaper in October 1964 it has enjoyed remarkable success. During two decades

115

which have seen print, paper and labour costs rise faster than inflation *Militant* has not just survived as a newspaper but has vastly expanded. It was a four-page monthly when it began on the eve of Labour's return to power in 1964. According to one of the founders, Terry Harrison, the starting funds were scraped together by the people involved, some of whom 'sold off family heirlooms'.[3] Most left-wing newspapers count themselves lucky if they survive beyond a few issues: it is rare for radical politicians to possess sufficient entrepreneurial flair, or simply enough money, to keep a paper going after the initial enthusiasm and funds have run out. But *Militant* has not just remained on its feet financially: it has prospered. Today it is a sixteen-page weekly, a substantial read, and in September 1983 the tendency launched an appeal for £150,000 to enable it to buy larger premises and eventually to publish *Militant* daily. It is ironic that Militant should be pressing ahead with such plans just as TUC and Labour Party leaders are claiming that the idea of a daily paper for the whole labour movement is unrealistic.

While *Militant*'s claimed circulation of 40,000 is almost certainly an exaggeration—20,000 would be more accurate— after the *New Statesman* the paper is probably the most popular left-wing weekly in Britain. But it would be wrong to spend too much time comparing the *Militant* newspaper with other journals. As we have seen, Militant is much more than just a newspaper: it is a large-scale political organization with more full-time staff than either the Liberal Party or the Social Democrats, and soon it may have as many employees as the Labour Party itself. So where does the money come from?

One source is obvious. Every week *Militant* carries a 'Fighting Fund' column in its pages, urging readers to send in money to help the paper. In the early days the Fund's target was to raise a modest £500 as soon as possible; today it aims to raise £50,000 every three months, though it is not always successful. £47,000 was received by the Fighting

Fund in 1977, £66,000 in 1978, £80,000 in 1979, £94,000 in 1980, £103,000 in 1981, £148,000 in 1982 and £152,000 in 1983.[4] Each week *Militant* carries news of the latest generous contributions, from 50p given by an old-age pensioner to thousands of pounds raised at one public meeting. A table shows how well each area is doing with respect to the target set for it. Any area which achieves its target in one quarter will get a higher one next time; areas that fail get the same target again. The Fund has in the past included donations from several Labour MPs, including Eddie Loyden (a *Militant* sympathizer in Liverpool)[5] and, in October 1974, Manchester MP Paul Rose, who sent £3 to thank Militant supporters for their help in his election campaign.[6] Rose described his Militant election workers in 1974 as 'a breath of fresh air'.[7] Seven years later he joined the SDP.

But even with revenue of more than £150,000 a year, the Fighting Fund alone could not possibly support an organization the size of Militant, whose electricity and phone bills are each around £20,000 a year (for the three main premises). There must be some other, more substantial, source of money.

It has frequently been suggested by Militant's critics that the tendency receives a foreign subsidy—the 'Moscow Gold' theory. How else could it keep going on sales and donations alone? it is asked. Examples of other left-wing papers that depend on foreign support are often quoted. The *Morning Star*, for instance, now down to a daily circulation of under 30,000, sells half its copies to Eastern Europe, and by all accounts Moscow newsagents do not sell out half-way through the morning rush-hour. The *Morning Star*'s reliance on the Soviet bloc has long been public knowledge. Less well-known until recently have been the links between Libya and certain left-wing papers in Britain. It is difficult to imagine what foreign power would want to subsidize *Militant*, though. Neither the Soviet Union nor Colonel

Gadafi's Libya would find it an attractive proposition, since the paper is highly critical of both their regimes.

Militant's only real international financial link is through its own committee for the Workers' International. But here Militant is exporting money, not bringing it into the country. Each section of the CWI has to pay £5 per member per year, and since Militant is about as big as all the other sections put together and has a very paternalistic attitude towards them, Militant subsidizes work in other countries. In recent years Militant has been making generous grants (tens of thousands of pounds a year) to its small section in the African National Congress in South Africa. The only financial benefit Militant seems to have gained from its international links was the printing of some of its pamphlets and books by the comrades in Sri Lanka in the early 1970s. In return for arranging the cheap printing, the Sri Lankans were allowed a few pages at the back of one pamphlet for an article by one of their members.[8]

The leaders of Militant vehemently deny any foreign source of funds, and I have found no evidence whatsoever that the tendency receives money from abroad. To understand where most of its money does come from one needs first to look at the tendency's formal financial organization.

Militant owns two limited companies, WIR Publications Limited and Cambridge Heath Press Limited. WIR Publications Limited was an 'off-the-shelf' £100 company incorporated in June 1973 with an ambitious object: 'to aid and further the interests of the international working class' and 'to render aid, pecuniary or otherwise, to labour or socialist candidates in parliamentary, municipal or other elections'.[9] This firm is clearly a continuation of previous RSL and Militant trading names dating back to the foundation of the *Workers' International Review* in 1956. The Revolutionary Socialist League ran a business (as opposed to a company) called Workers' International Review (Publishers), which in

1963 seems to have become WIR Publications (again not a company), the predecessor of the present firm.

Cambridge Heath Press Limited, the earlier of the two companies, was incorporated in August 1971. Presumably it was named after Cambridge Heath Road in Bethnal Green, where Militant had bought premises and installed their new printing press only a few months before. Cambridge Heath Press has the aims of a printing and publishing company.[10]

As limited companies, both firms are legally obliged to lodge up-to-date lists of directors and shareholders with Companies House in the City and to submit annual accounts.

Journalists and Militant's enemies have spent hours hunched over the microfilm projectors in the Public Search Room at Companies House, trying to make something out of the records of these two companies. They do make interesting reading. WIR Publications Limited, for instance, has twenty-five people listed as its original shareholders: Robert Reeves, Raymond Apps, Robert Faulkes, Robert Edwards, Robert McKee, Terence Harrison, Michael Newman, Edward Mooney, Anthony Mulhearn, Thomas Ward, Lynn Walsh, Robin Jamieson, Peter Doyle, Alan Woods, Muriel Browning, Pat Wall, Brian Beckingham, William Webster, Peter Hadden, Alex Wood, Terence Wilson, Pat Craven, Clare Doyle, Ted Grant and Keith Dickinson. Patrick Craven was the first Company Secretary.[11] The list is virtually a roll of honour of the big names of Militant and seems to correspond to the Central (National) Committee when the company was set up in 1973, when Patrick Craven was treasurer of the RSL. Recently it was being suggested that these names should provide the list of those to be expelled from the Labour Party. That would have been rather unfair, since at least one of those named, Alex Wood, is no longer involved in Militant. In 1980, three years after Wood had left the tendency, Clare Doyle wrote to ask him to send his one share back. Wood duly obliged, unaware perhaps that the certificate might have fetched a good price in some circles.

What of the accounts themselves? Can these provide the answer to the Militant riches? The first person to analyse them in any detail was a solicitor and Labour Party member, Charles James. The event that sparked off his work was a petty incident which occurred in 1976, when James was chairman of an LPYS branch in mid-Bedfordshire. At a regional Young Socialists' conference Militant's organizer for the Eastern Region had criticized James's branch for not being 'political enough'. What he meant, of course, was that the branch did not support Militant. Charles James was so annoyed by this attack that he resolved to discover as much as he could about Militant's financial background and to publicize his findings. In the next few months James spent many hours at Companies House, and even more time in the library at the London School of Economics, going through the collection of *Militant* back numbers on microfilm. He was aided by his training as a lawyer, and contacts with one or two Militant defectors pointed him in the right direction. The result of James's work was a series of reports, each entitled 'The Companies We Keep', the first of which came out in 1977. Each was passed on to officials in Labour's regional and head offices, and at least one edition reached the then leader, Jim Callaghan. Several journalists were also given copies, and the information was used in newspaper and television reports. All Charles James's discoveries were based on public information produced by Militant itself, either in returns to Companies House or in the pages of the *Militant* newspaper. His work eventually helped to lead to the simple (and, to some people, disappointing) answer to the question of where Militant gets most of its money.

Charles James discovered that one of the two Militant companies, WIR Publications Limited, seemed to be making regular loans to the other, Cambridge Heath Press Limited: in the year 1976 £50,000 was lent, in 1977, £48,500; in 1978,

£50,000; in 1979, £66,966; in 1980, £89,236; in 1981, £119,000 and in 1982, £173,000.[12] At first they were simple loans due for repayment in 1986, but now they have been converted into mortgage debentures. The companies' accountants, Norton, Shaw and Nathan, have said in the annual accounts that they consider the money 'may be irrecoverable'[13]. By 1982 the total amount loaned by WIR Publications Limited to its sister company was £596,702. So while *Militant* is officially published and printed by Cambridge Heath Press Limited, much of its income is effectively coming from WIR Publications Limited. In short, WIR Publications acts as a collecting box for Cambridge Heath Press. This arrangement was made 'on advice from lawyers and accountants':[14] if the *Militant* newspaper got into libel difficulties, only the official publisher, Cambridge Heath Press, could be sued (along with certain individuals), and any money in WIR Publications would remain untouchable. That sum is considerable. According to its accounts, WIR Publications received £18,000 income in the year 1974, £30,000 in 1975, £42,000 in 1976, £61,000 in 1977, £77,000 in 1978, £92,000 in 1979, £114,000 in 1980 and £147,000 in 1981.[15]

But until 1980 it was not certain where these donations to WIR Publications were coming from in the first place. The answer was suddenly provided by Militant itself, perhaps to dampen the mounting speculation prompted by the work of Charles James and others. In April 1980, in reply to a questionnaire from the NEC of the Labour Party, Peter Taaffe said that WIR Publications Limited's income was 'derived solely from the donations of active members of the Labour Party and trade unions who, in addition to occasional donations to the *Militant* Fighting Fund, are prepared to make regular contributions to develop the support for Marxist policies within the labour movement'.[16] In other words, WIR's income was coming simply from Militant members and supporters. In saying this Taaffe was admitting for the first time that the Militant Fighting Fund was not the only source of donations from individuals. It was a remarkable statement, since anybody reading the exhortations every week in the Fighting Fund column in *Militant* would quite naturally have assumed that the paper's survival depended entirely on the Fund. Close examination shows, however, that names in the column are always 'unknowns' in Militant terms. They are almost exclusively those of people who are regular readers but not yet heavily involved in the tendency: the 'contacts' and 'contact members'. The column in *Militant* is used to encourage them; names are included not according to the size of donations but on the recommendation of local full-timers who want to entice potential recruits. When names appear in print the full-timers will make a big thing of it and make the 'contacts' feel important.

The case of one Militant ex-member from the early 1970s illustrates this. Richard Hart's name appeared in the Fighting Fund column on a number of occasions in early 1973.[17] At that point, Hart now admits, he was undergoing the 'contact' process. Later in the year, when Hart had become a full Militant member, his name no longer appeared in the column. As his bank statements show, he was by then making a regular £5 monthly banker's order payment to WIR Publications instead. This was his subscription.

All Militant defectors confirm that they had to pay regular and large subscriptions, though, unlike Hart, many paid weekly and in cash. There are no set subscription rates, only minimum levels: in general people are obliged to pay between 10 and 15 per cent of their income. 'I never knew how much anybody else paid,' remembers one defector. 'It was always a thing between you and the treasurer.'[18] Today a member on an average weekly wage of about £130 might have to pay about £15 a week: one member says that he paid £55 a month when he was earning £100 a week at Ford.[19] The higher-paid members pay astonishing sums—as much as £60 a week for those earning more than £10,000 a year. Students can expect to have to pay about £4 a week nowadays, with an extra £10 lump sum when grant cheques come through at the start of term. People still at school are asked for a large share of their pocket money—25p out of his weekly £1, one ex-member told me. Even the unemployed are asked to pay a minimum of £4 a week. It all makes the Labour Party's 1984 subscription of £7 a year look minute.

Large though Militant's subscriptions are, they are not the only sums that members have to fork out: they are constantly being badgered for extra money. As one ex-member put it:

> You know when you're at a Militant 'social': you pay to get in, you pay for food, booze, raffle tickets, even pamphlets and books; then there's a Fighting Fund collection; and if your pockets aren't empty by then, somebody's bound to tip you upside-down to make sure your coffers are bare when you leave. I know people who used to hide their last 30p so they could get home on the bus.[20]

Members are always expected to be the first to contribute to Fighting Fund collections at Young Socialist and public meetings. In many cases Militant branch treasurers will go round and arrange beforehand exactly who will make large contributions to encourage the rest. IOUs are discouraged because they cause branch treasurers so much trouble in following people up, but in the end a pledge is regarded as better than nothing. At the LPYS Conference in 1982, £8,000 was raised at the Militant fringe meeting (although the target had been £10,000).[21] Sometimes when the organization is in deficit extra money will be collected from each member in a nationwide branch levy. For instance, in December 1982 each member was asked to pay a sum corresponding to twice his weekly subscription, and people were warned this might be done again in future.[22] Members who get tax rebates are always expected to donate all of them to the cause, and the organization occasionally receives bequests in wills, though because the membership is mainly young the benefits of this have yet to be fully realized.

Activity in trade unions is another important source of funds from Militant members. Members of the tendency who serve on union conference delegations often receive generous overnight allowances for the time that they are away from home, as do full-time union officials. The Civil Service union, the CPSA, in which Militant has been strong for some time, pays an allowance of £32 a night when members are away on union business. Recently the union has had in important positions several Militant members, many of whom live outside London but frequently have to visit the capital for union matters. Militant's finances have thus benefited from the several thousands of pounds contributed by CPSA officials and union delegates who choose to take cheap accommodation and donate most of their allowances to Militant. (It should be stressed that there is nothing illegal or irregular about this.)

Only part of the money raised from members goes to London or appears in the accounts of WIR Publications Limited. Probably about a quarter of Militant's income is retained at the local level to pay for full-timers and other expenses. Each region, district and branch has its own budget and bank account. In Lancashire, for example, Militant has a bank account in Blackburn under the name of the Lancashire Book Club.[23] The rest of each subscription is sent on to the Militant financial office at 300 Mare Street in Hackney. Presumably accountants have advised Militant that diverse national and regional bank accounts will help to avoid any unnecessary tax payments. They also mislead people doing investigations based on the returns at Companies House.

Apart from the Fighting Fund, members' subscriptions

124

and other donations, there are several other important sources of income for the tendency.

First, there are sales of the *Militant* newspaper. Around 20,000 copies are sold per week—including twelve subscriptions to the Metropolitan Police and one to the US Embassy. Paper sales should theoretically bring in about £4,000 a week in all or £200,000 a year, but Militant suffers from quite a severe leakage among sellers who genuinely forget to hand the money in. In some cases members will pay money in without having sold their quota of papers, so as to avoid criticism or the trouble of having to stand on a street corner selling them. Sometimes the paper will be given away to 'good types' if they cannot afford to buy it. The organization does not count paper sales as a particularly important or reliable source of income. The paper is regarded more a means of spreading the gospel.

Second, the bookshop at Mentmore Terrace brings in money. Under the business name of World Socialist Books (formerly World Books), it sells a wide range of books and pamphlets—not just Militant or Marxist literature—and its titles include books from many leading publishers. All Militant members are expected to buy their set texts and books from the shop, and members even have to pay 30p for internal documents such as the annual 'British Perspectives and Tasks'. Militant never misses an opportunity to raise extra cash. But since World Socialist Books is not a limited company, it is impossible to assess its turnover.

The third source of income is commercial printing. Over the last few years income from this has greatly increased. In February 1983, when Peter Tatchell got into trouble with Walworth Road for using Cambridge Heath Press to print his election leaflets, it was revealed that sixty local Labour parties in London alone had used Cambridge Heath Press as a printer at one time or another. As Tatchell explained: 'We did this not out of political sympathy with Militant but because they were fast, cheap and knew what we wanted. More important, they were a trade union shop, and all the workers were Labour Party members.'[24]

Militant tries to ensure that the Labour Party bodies it controls always place their printing orders with Cambridge Heath Press. Added together, the value of these orders can be considerable. For instance, in 1977–8 the London region of NOLS, controlled by Militant, had a total expenditure of £269.71. Of this £178.90 was spent on printing with Cambridge Heath Press and a further £8 went on advertising in *Militant*—a total of £186.90.[25] In other words, nearly 70 per cent of the NOLS region's spending went to the tendency. The sums may have been small in that case, but the same thing was going on in many other LPYS and NOLS bodies. It is all part of a strategy by Militant effectively to integrate the finances of the tendency with those of the Labour Party bodies that it controls, allowing the former to be subsidized by the latter. In recent years party officials have tried to stop some of these bodies from using Militant for Labour Party printing work, and most LPYS and NOLS print work now goes elsewhere. Instead Militant is doing an increasing amount of work for left-wing pressure groups, many of which have no association with the Labour Party, and for unions. Militant prints several of the CPSA's sectional magazines, for instance. And it is not just socialists who find Militant's printing rates competitive: in 1983 a local Conservative association even used Cambridge Heath Press, unaware of the company's identity.

In the 1960s the tendency's internal motto was 'The Three Ps—Premises, Press and Professionals', Militant's three organizational ambitions. It is a measure of Militant's growth since then that each aim has been achieved several times over. But of the three the press is perhaps the most important because of its financial advantages. Militant bought its first press in 1971, helped partly by donations from two members of the then Militant Executive, Roger and Julian Silverman. They had just inherited a large sum from their father, Sydney Silverman, the left-wing MP for Nelson and Colne, who died in 1968, leaving £63,548. Within fifteen months of acquiring that first press the paper had progressed from being a four-page monthly to an eight-page weekly and had adopted a colour logo. The paper has expanded rapidly since then, along with the organization, and today Militant has three big presses in its London offices.

Now that it has its own printing facilities Militant no longer has to rely on outsiders and can make money from doing commercial printing for others. But, most important, it has cut the costs of printing its own literature. Other printers' rates not only include a profit margin for themselves but also allow for labour paid at union rates. Although its print workers are members of the relevant print unions, the NGA and SOGAT '82, and their journalists belong to the National Union of Journalists (NUJ), Militant does not, in effect, pay them at union rates. Of course, when asked, Militant always says that its staff get standard rates of pay; what it forgets to add is that every member of the newspaper and printing staff chooses not to take his or her full wages—the amount they forgo is a donation to Militant. Though Militant itself campaigns publicly for the introduction of a £100 minimum wage, all Militant's staff—print workers, journalists and organizers—receive much less than this. But if Militant employees choose to give back some of their nominal income, there is nothing that the NUJ or the print unions can do about it.

Wages for full-time staff vary according to rank and needs. Those who are single may get as little as £40 a week; those with a spouse and children, up to £80. The partners of Militant employees are always encouraged to take well-paid jobs elsewhere to support their spouses' meagre earnings. And only just over half the current full-time staff of more than 130 people are paid in any case: as I have noted, the rest rely on state benefits, though in some cases Militant adds to these.

It is not easy to put a figure to Militant's total annual turnover from both members and other sources. Although Militant defectors know about their own contributions during their time in the organization, even those formerly in important positions know very little about overall figures. This is for reasons of security: there is no cause for ordinary members to be told.

The total income raised simply from the members' subscriptions can only be estimated, but my calculation is that it is at least £750,000 a year, and that is probably on the low side: 4,700 members paying a minimum of £5 a week works out at more than £1 million a year, but I have reduced this estimate to allow for people who fail to pay even the minimum, such as those at school and those on state benefits, though many members pay much more than £5 a week. Add to that revenue from the sales of *Militant* and other publications (at least £150,000), donations to the Fighting Fund (£148,000 in 1982) and profits from commercial printing work (probably at least £100,000), and one arrives at a figure for total income of somewhere between £1 million and £1¼ million.

This figure seems to be very high, but in my view is probably an under-estimate. It is confirmed by the evidence of a recent defector, Michael Gregory, who reported that in 1982 approximately £500,000 had been raised by the Centre by 24 October of that year.[26] Allowing for the retention of a certain amount of money locally, for an increase in the number of Militant members since then and in the minimum subscription (from £4 to £5), for inflation, for the usual late surge in fund-raising towards the end of the year and for the fact that there were still ten weeks to go, it would be reasonable to calculate that for the year 1983 the total income of the tendency would be in the region I suggest.

With financial resources on this scale, the question one has to ask is: where does all the money go? First, salaries and National Insurance must account for £300,000 or £400,000 a year. Second, the *Militant* newspaper is not commercially viable and has to be subsidized—the costs of printing and distribution are by no means balanced by sales and the small amount of advertising revenue. Militant's internal documents must be costly too. On top of that there are rents and rates on Militant's properties, telephone, electricity and gas bills and day-to-day administrative expenses. A very large amount of money goes towards subsidizing Militant's operations abroad.

How does Militant's turnover compare with those of other political parties and pressure groups? Calculating annual income or expenditure figures for political parties can be difficult, as the Houghton Inquiry found out in 1976.[27] While records are kept of national income and expenditure, no party keeps central records of the finances of each constituency. There is also the danger of double-counting money that passes from the local level to the centre. For the calendar year 1982, not an election year, a very rough estimate of total Labour Party income is about £5 million.[28] The Liberals estimate their total income for the same year to be around £1½ million.[29] The Social Democrats' estimate is about £1¼ million for their first year, 1981–2, and this is likely to drop to about £1 million for 1983–4.[30] So the income of Militant is almost as high as that of the Liberal Party and about the same as the SDP's, although the comparison is not entirely appropriate, since these parties do not make money from commercial printing and publishing operations. Perhaps Militant has something to teach them here.

By comparison simply with internal Labour Party pressure groups, Militant is in a totally different league. The Fabian Society's income for the year ending June 1983 was

£81,000.[31] *Tribune* has an annual income of about £140,000,[32] while the influential Campaign for Labour Party Democracy had an income of £14,494 in the twelve months to October 1983.[33] Militant may try to argue that it is merely another Labour Party pressure group, but its finances are at the level of those of a major political party.

8

The Militant Life

At the start of the 1970s Militant still had only between 100 and 200 members. The really big jump in membership occurred during the following five years, after Militant had taken over the LPYS. In 1971 membership was such that the Militant annual conference was held in a pub in London. By January 1975 the tendency had 600 members, and later that year, when the annual gathering was held at a proper conference centre, Owen's Park in Manchester, Ted Grant is reported to have got up and announced proudly that membership had now soared past the thousand mark. 'The first thousand is the hard thing,' Grant apparently told the cheering delegates. 'The next thousand will be easier and ten thousand easier still.'[1]

Grant's announcement was probably premature, but Militant's control of the LPYS was clearly paying dividends. From about the mid-1970s, however, there seems to have been a significant fall in the 'quality' of Militant membership. In the early days, when Militant's membership numbered only a few hundred people, each new recruit had to be properly 'steeled in the ideas'. It usually took at least six months for a 'contact' to go through the recruitment process—sometimes as much as eighteen months, especially for those who were middle-class. Peter Taaffe used to say of 'middle-class types': 'They should be dried in the wind, buried in the snow, fried on the grill, then dried in the wind and buried in the snow again, and then, and only then, we might accept them.'[2]

In the very early days, during the 1960s, all new recruits would travel to the Militant headquarters in London to be approved in person by Grant or Taaffe before being accepted as members. By the early 1970s the organization was becoming so large that this was no longer possible, but even then new members would be visited by Central Committee members. As membership expanded still further and the annual targets became increasingly ambitious, full-timers and branches started cutting corners to bring in new recruits. By 1979 there were 1,800 members; by November 1981, 2,500; by November 1982, 3,500; and 4,700 at the end of 1983. People did not have to go through anything like the same process to join, and standards dropped—so much so that nowadays it may be only a matter of weeks before potential recruits become members. The result is that not only are they less well educated in, and less committed to, Militant's ideas but they also feel less privileged to be part of the tendency. Since the mid-1970s Militant has suffered from a constant stream of embarrassing defectors, many of whom have spoken to Labour Party officials and the press. In the twenty years of its existence more than 1,200 people have left the tendency or have been expelled. In researching this book I have managed to talk to fifteen of those former members, from different periods and from different levels of the organization. Some were unwilling to be named, but others were happy to be quoted.

David Mason works as an accountant for the Fabian Society at its head office in London. He was a member of Militant in Hull and Birmingham for about eighteen months in the mid-1970s. He was not with Militant long enough to become very important, but his case is typical of those of many young people who join the tendency.

Mason joined the Labour Party in October 1974 after working for Labour during that month's election campaign. As a young recruit he quite naturally began going to local LPYS meetings in Hull. Soon he came across Alastair Tice, a Militant member, who sold him copies of the paper and started discussing politics with him. Often after a meeting they would go to the pub and talk, or they would arrange to go out for a drink on a Friday evening. Sometimes Tice would bring along friends from other Young Socialist branches in Hull. He gave Mason Militant pamphlets and books to read; they soon started discussing Marxism, and the meetings became more regular. From the pub they would often go back to Tice's home and carry on talking politics well into the night:

> After about a month of fairly intensive discussion, Alastair broke the news to me that there was this organization, the Revolutionary Socialist League. He gave me copies of 'British Perspectives and Tasks' and 'World Perspectives' and the pamphlet 'Entrism', all of which I took away and read. Then we discussed them, and after about a month I was accepted into membership.[3]

Reflecting on it now, Mason admits that at the time the arguments put forward by Tice and his friends 'seemed quite reasonable'. And, importantly, Mason got on well with them. He found the rest of the left in the Hull Labour Party 'weak and flabby': Militant and the Young Socialists were the only group to challenge the local party's right-wing leadership.

Mason started attending meetings of the Hull Militant branch, which were held every week in the back room of the Minerva pub, situated at the end of what was then the pier from which the boats to Grimsby used to leave. The branch had about a dozen members, drawn from the three Hull constituencies and from the university Labour Club. The set-up was very formal, with a chairman, treasurer and secretary and other ad hoc officers; minutes were read at the start of each meeting. Mason himself was later appointed Irish organizer for the branch, which meant that he had to talk about Ireland at local Labour Party and Young Socialist meetings and at private and public meetings of Militant. The officers were elected by the branch itself, but every time it was obvious to Mason who was going to get which job.

Soon Mason himself became involved in the slow recruitment of new members. He was assigned a small paper round of four or five 'contacts'. Every week he had to sell each of them a copy of the paper and discuss politics. The procedure was exactly the same as the one through which he himself had gone only a few weeks before. At the weekly branch meeting each member had to report back on how his or her 'contacts' were progressing: if they looked good, the branch would vote on whether to accept them into membership. Then, after the minutes, the officers' reports and instructions and news on 'contacts', a member of the branch had to lead off a political discussion:

> At only my second or third meeting I had to introduce the discussion. My talk was on Trotsky's 'Transitional Programme'. Everybody who had just joined got the 'Transitional Programme' because it was easy, but slowly you got harder and harder things to speak on. Nothing beyond you, though—every subject was chosen to stretch you a little bit more. You did a lot of preparation for them.[4]

Mason lasted about a year and a half in Militant, but in the end he left because of policy disagreements. He could not accept the tendency's policy on Ireland, and Stuart Holland's book *The Socialist Challenge* persuaded him that there were other forms of socialism:

It wasn't a big bust-up. I announced I had disagreements. They said it was politically inept. They tried to keep me in and agreed to let me make a 'Why I Want to Leave' speech. Then at its next meeting the branch voted on whether I should be expelled or not. I was told not to turn up. The decision was that I should remain a nominal member—in effect it was a suspension. Their theory was that when the 'Perspectives' were one day fulfilled I'd want to come back in. But then I wrote an article in *Labour Weekly* defending import controls, and I was finally expelled for publicly opposing Militant policy. I had to give back my main documents, and they asked if I would go to the press about it. I didn't. Later when I was elected to NOLS National Committee, Andy Bevan revealed that I'd been a Militant supporter just to cause trouble for me on the National Committee.[5]

Today, eight years later, David Mason remembers that on the whole his life in Militant was 'unending tedium':

A lot of it boiled down to selling papers. The pace didn't bother me, but one day I suddenly realized that after a year my social circle had totally drifted. I had only political friends left, simply because of the lack of time. There'd be the Militant branch on Monday evening, the Young Socialists meeting another evening, 'contact' work on Friday night, selling papers on Sunday afternoon, and on top of that, to prove to the local Labour Party we were good party members, we went canvassing for them every week and worked like hell in the local elections.[6]

Terry McDonald was a member of Militant in the tendency's home patch, Liverpool. Like many other defectors, his membership was brief—about eighteen months. After leaving Militant he soon left the Labour Party and joined the Social Democrats. In the circumstances this is perhaps understandable. It can't be particularly easy to be an ex-member of

Militant and carry on as a Labour Party activist on Mersey-side.

McDonald works for Knowsley Borough Council and became involved with the tendency through his union, NALGO. Although NALGO is not affiliated to the Labour Party, the Knowsley NALGO branch contains a number of Militant members, thanks to the work of Derek Hatton, a community relations officer in the borough and now deputy leader of Liverpool council. Through Hatton, McDonald started going to NALGO *Militant* readers meetings and later to his ward Labour Party in the then Kirkdale constituency of Liverpool. There followed the usual series of chats in local pubs until McDonald was told: 'We have this group which meets and has discussions about party matters.' McDonald says:

> It didn't surprise me. I knew there was some sort of caucus. They invited me to the next meeting, so I went along to this house in Anfield. When I got there I was shocked. There was a table set up at the top of the room with a chairman, secretary, minutes secretary and treasurer—it was just like a Labour Party meeting.[7]

Militant always advises members not to take on positions in the Labour Party which require a lot of donkey work. In most cases members are advised simply to go for party positions with political influence, such as Youth Officer and Political Education Officer. Because of Militant's strength in his local party in Kirkdale, McDonald quickly found that after joining Militant there were no problems about a career in the Kirkdale Labour Party or his union:

> I fought the council elections three times. I was made ward chairman, constituency party chairman, district Labour Party delegate and I was treasurer of my union branch. The higher tier of Militant had obviously decided that I was suitable for these posts, and so I got them.[8]

136

And McDonald soon got over his initial shock:

> I was told at the start that we didn't ever mention this group had ever met. You weren't supposed to ask questions. It was frowned upon. But I was flattered. You were one of the chosen few. A lot of those who joined were just looking for a cause.[9]

Like all Militant members, McDonald became involved in the search for others looking for a cause:

> We were always being told to look out for 'good types'. Part of the business at branch meetings was 'Any good types?'. You'd say so-and-so spoke well at a union meeting. 'Really?' they'd say. 'See if he'll second this motion.' The next week I'd go back and tell them he had seconded it. 'That's interesting.' So then one of the officers would make contact with him, and it went from there.[10]

McDonald remembers life in Militant as a 'series of tests'. Members were given a quota of papers to sell each week but often ended up paying for them with their own money instead. He also recalls the political education: 'One week you'd get the latest "Perspectives" document. Next week the members were tested on it. "You didn't read page four," they'd accuse you.'[11]

In the end McDonald left Militant in anger at its attitude towards other Labour Party members who were not in the tendency:

> Several new people joined my ward. They were true socialists but were treated shabbily by Militant and were verbally abused. Just because their motions were deemed to be 'unacceptable', they weren't getting through. I started to question this. These people had worked hard for me in the council elections. In the end it came to a meeting

in a pub in Huyton with Derek Hatton. I told him they were too doctrinaire and that I was unhappy about these people who were 'real socialists'. I was told I'd lose all my positions, that I'd be a 'non-person' as far as the Labour Party was concerned.[12]

And that's exactly what happened. In the months that followed his departure from Militant, McDonald failed to get re-elected to the posts that Militant had once secured for him. The only position he did retain—thanks to some clever footwork—was the chairmanship of the Kirkdale constituency party. But when McDonald started speaking to the press about his time in Militant and giving television interviews, he says that the Militant supporters in his party made his position unbearable. In the end he gave up and left the Labour Party altogether.

Richard Hart joined Militant in March 1973, seven years after joining the Labour Party, and was a member of a branch in south London. There he shared a house at 13 Elsiemaud Road in Deptford, which became a sort of Militant household, with several leading Militant people as tenants. The building was also used for Marxist discussion meetings and for putting people up when they came to London: 'Keith Dickinson used to say you should give up your bed for members of the National Committee, because they were working hard all week.'[13] At one point the Labour Party was so suspicious about the fact that several Militant supporters were living in the same building that it carried out an inquiry into 13 Elsiemaud Road, but investigations revealed nothing more sinister than several like-minded friends sharing the same house.

Hart left Militant in the end for several reasons. One was that he got married; another was the conflict between his work for Militant and his job as a librarian:

138

I told them I couldn't help out on Saturdays because of my job. They felt I was using my job as an excuse not to do more work for the tendency and they held it up to ridicule. I was told that my job wasn't really all that important, and that the tendency is. They didn't regard it as a useful job in the community. I was told to fake migraine, but I thought this was dishonest and so I didn't. Then that summer I found I was addressing a meeting and coming out with all their phrases. I no longer felt an independent person. I felt sucked into them and started feeling the tendency could take over my whole life.[14]

Mike Barnes was a member of Militant in the mid-1970s, first in Edinburgh, when he was at school, and later in York, when he was at university. He is now a film director with the BBC in Scotland.

Barnes was recruited in exactly the same way as everybody else. When he was a member of the Young Socialists in Edinburgh the local Militant branch had allocated members to talk to him about politics and to report on progress:

Eventually the great day came when the Organization was revealed to me, followed by an invitation to internal meetings. I was sworn to secrecy and, with a feeling of being involved in something very important, agreed to attend.[15]

It was a secret spy-like world. There was tremendous excitement about it all and tremendous attraction at first.[16]

Barnes agrees with many ex-defectors that, as well as helping prevent expulsion from the Labour Party, this secrecy contributes to the 'cohesion, sense of self-importance and siege mentality'.[17]

The most abiding memories of life in Militant are filled

with the sheer strain of it all. If you were even moderately active, you would be asked to attend up to six or seven boring meetings in one week.[18]

You built up an alternative set of social contacts as much as political activity. It can easily take over people's lives. It became obsessive. They were almost inventing meetings to attend. There was a ridiculous number of meetings held to discuss such a small amount of work. Even if you didn't have a meeting one evening, you'd end up drinking with them.[19]

The kind of commitment that Militant required was bundled together in the form of highly alienating personal relationships. You had to make sure your subscriptions were paid and your papers sold so as not to feel guilty when you chatted to other members. The only way out seemed to be 'family commitments' and the unspoken truth that as soon as a young Militant member got a girlfriend he either recruited her or left.[20]

Barnes particularly remembers how difficult it was to be a member of Militant and a student:

When I was at York University there was this attitude that students weren't really proper members—which only added to our guilt feelings. The important thing, we were told, was to get workers involved—people from the town. So you had all these students trying to do their bit by chatting up railway workers and buying them drinks in the hope they would buy a copy of the paper. Then you had the horrible thing of going round a council estate on a Sunday afternoon trying to sell papers. We all hated it, but nobody dared admit it.[21]

Mike Barnes eventually left because of policy differences. He soon tired of reading Militant's set texts—Marx, Lenin and Grant ('easily the most boring writer in the entire far left')—and began to explore other Marxist literature. Soon the gulf between Militant's position and the Labour Party's became just too wide.

> I sent them a long letter to say why I was resigning. So they brought in the full-timers and I was persuaded into having a chat in the university bar. It went on all night and we ended up in someone's room. It really turned into a theological argument and one full-timer turned to me and said, 'You've lost your *faith* in the working class.' This was after an evening during which I'd been saying it was all religious and they'd been denying it.[22]

The similarities between Militant and a religion are obvious from the lifestyle of the members. One has only to attend a large public Militant rally to notice the parallels with a Billy Graham meeting. Militant's set texts are treated like the Bible, and quotations from Trotsky and Marx are used in the same way as biblical extracts. Meetings on political matters are more a matter of teaching the members about Marx, Trotsky and Lenin than of developing any new thought. Members are tested on the set texts as if they were Holy Writ. Militant's simple political philosophy has an appeal to a certain type of person because, like a religion, it answers life's problems. As Mike Barnes points out, there is tremendous faith in the working class and an almost inexplicable optimism about the eventual demise of capitalism. The full-timer plays the role of the priest, interpreting the teachings passed down from on high and dealing with the problems of individual members of his congregation.

What happens to members of Militant when they leave? Most of the ex-members I have met are still involved in Labour politics, but it was far more likely that I would come across ex-members still in politics than those who had given it up. My estimate is that about half leave politics altogether, although they may return later, and most retain left-wing sympathies. Many who stay in the Labour Party go on to pursue orthodox careers—several former members of Militant stood as Labour candidates at the last election (for example, Ian Pearson in Bexhill and Battle, Martin Upham in Harborough, Alex Wood in Edinburgh West and Jake Magee in Uxbridge). There seems to be no real trend in the political direction of ex-members. Mike Barnes says that his political views now probably correspond most closely with those of the Socialist Workers' Party, and others I have met still call themselves Marxists. Some defectors are now on the Bennite left of the Labour Party, while others, such as Mason and McDonald, have moved well to the right.

9

Militant Merseyside

In the June 1983 election the City of Liverpool was the one place that stood out against the Tory tide. While Britain as a whole recorded a swing of 3.9 per cent from Labour to the Conservatives, Liverpool saw a swing of 2.4 per cent from Conservative to Labour, and for the first time in recent history Liverpool had no Conservative MPs. A similar trend had occurred in the local elections five weeks earlier. While the Conservatives had made small gains in town halls across the country—so persuading Mrs Thatcher to call the general election—to the surprise of many concerned, for the first time in ten years Liverpool elected a Labour Council. But then in politics, as in so many things, Liverpool has always been different.

Liverpool has played an important part in the history of Militant. It is the city where the tendency really began and where it has been most successful. So far this book has been concerned with the development and organization of Militant at a national level, but in order to understand how Militant operates and has succeeded at the local level it is worth taking a trip to Merseyside.

Over a period of fourteen months, between February 1981 and March 1982, the public face of the Labour Party in Liverpool underwent a remarkable transformation. Three of the party's MPs—Richard Crawshaw, Eric Ogden and

Jimmy Dunn—all defected to the Social Democrats, making Liverpool an SDP stronghold, at least for the time being. Eric Ogden left after being dropped by his constituency party in the new reselection process introduced by the Labour Party in 1980. Crawshaw and Dunn went before reselection had taken place, but for both men there was a very strong possibility that they would not be chosen again.

At the same time the Liverpool party selected a new generation of left-wing candidates—four of them Militant members. First, Terry Harrison, a Militant founder, was picked to fight Edge Hill, a Labour seat until 1979. Taking over from Crawshaw in Toxteth was a print worker, Tony Mulhearn, chairman of the Liverpool District Labour Party. In Kirkdale Labour chose Terry Fields, a member of the Executive of the Fire Brigades' Union. And finally in the Conservative seat of Wavertree they picked a young, energetic Militant councillor, Derek Hatton.

In the event only one of those four candidates, Terry Fields, actually stood in June 1983. Boundary changes reduced the number of Liverpool seats from eight to six, and with the threat of expulsions Militant wisely saw the redistribution as an opportunity to cool it a bit, and so three of its candidates withdrew. On election night, though, Terry Fields was elected MP for Liverpool Broadgreen and could boast of a 4.8 per cent swing to Labour.

Labour's earlier success in the 1983 Liverpool Council elections was heralded by both Liberals and Conservatives as a success not so much for Labour as for Militant. Naturally Militant agreed with this interpretation. For several years the tendency has been the dominant faction within the Liverpool District Labour Party and an influential minority in the Council Labour group. So powerful is the tendency on Merseyside that it has its own premises and at least six full-time organizers. The Liverpool Labour Party has just one full-time employee. According to one leading local Labour official, 'Militant effectively runs the Liverpool Labour Party.'

Most people in Liverpool Labour politics, whatever their political position, agree on one point: the tendency's success can be explained partly by Merseyside's appalling economic conditions. Several older right-wing members of the party say that if they were now unemployed teenagers, they would find Militant attractive.

Economically Merseyside suffered long before many parts of Britain knew what unemployment was. Liverpool—sometimes called the 'Bermuda Triangle' of British capitalism—cannot remember what it was like *without* the dole queues. Even in the days when it was a prosperous port thousands of men had to wander down to the docks every morning to bid for casual work. In the 1970s, as successive recessions hit the rest of Britain, Merseyside's problems multiplied. Of the ten constituencies in England and Wales with the worst unemployment in the 1981 census, four were in Liverpool, all with jobless rates of more than 25 per cent.[1] Now some parts of the city have more than 50 per cent unemployed. Liverpudlians were not shocked when riots broke out in Toxteth in 1981: what surprised them was that trouble had not occurred before. Extreme economic conditions may be expected to encourage extreme politics.

In 1934 a young Liberal graduate came to Liverpool to work in a shipping company: 'I saw there for the first time in my young life, with my own eyes, what poverty meant.... I saw mass unemployment as the most fearful curse which could befall our people.'[2] Michael Foot's experience persuaded him to become a socialist and to join the Labour Party. Fifty years later unemployment in the same city is driving today's young idealists to join Militant.

But Merseyside's economic plight cannot provide the only reason for Militant's success. Other parts of Britain have suffered just as much as Merseyside—Scotland and the

North-East, for example—without anything like the same support for Militant. And while revolutionary and Marxist groups have always been strong on Merseyside, it is only recently that they have succeeded in the Labour Party. For most of its history the Labour Party in Liverpool has been a very right-wing body, but in itself this partly explains Militant's recent success.

Only in recent times have Liverpool politics ceased to be dominated by religion. Until the 1920s the main opposition to the Conservatives had been not Labour but the Irish Nationalists, who even had a Liverpool MP. The Nationalists could always count on the Roman Catholic vote, but with the partition of Ireland in 1921 the party soon died out, and nearly all its members and supporters switched to Labour. This meant that the Labour Party was dominated by Catholics until after the Second World War and in the 1930s and 1940s was run by a Catholic machine. But as only about a quarter of Liverpool voters were Catholic, such an overwhelmingly Catholic party could never take over the town hall. Rather than vote Labour, many working-class Protestants supported the Working Men's Conservative Association, and it was not until 1955 that Labour gained full control of Liverpool Council. Liverpool University lecturer Tony Lane believes the Catholic inheritance created a style of Labour politics which has lasted ever since:

> There has always been a flavour of Tammany Hall about the Labour Party in Liverpool. . . . Where in other parts of Britain the Labour Party fell heir to the radical wing of the Liberal Party, no such process took place in Liverpool. The Labour Party, instead of inheriting the democratic, non-conformist tradition of the Liberal Party, acquired the conspiratorialism of Irish politics as practised in England.[3]

After the Second World War the Labour Party was dominated by the Braddocks. Jack Braddock was Labour leader on Liverpool Council, while his wife Bessie served as MP for Liverpool Exchange. The Braddocks in Liverpool have provided the best example of local boss politics in Labour Party history: the *New Statesman* once compared Liverpool with Chicago, calling the city 'Cook County, UK'.[4] People who applied to join the Labour Party in the Braddock era were often told it was 'full up'[5] at a time when membership in Liverpool was among the lowest in the country. 'The organization was poor and intentionally kept poor to keep out the "wrong" sort of candidate,' one official remarked later.[6] The decrepit organization bequeathed by Braddock survived until the late 1970s, providing an ideal opportunity for Militant. It is not difficult to win control of a party with very few members, of whom only a handful turn up to meetings. Once Militant has taken over, it is more than likely that many existing members will stop attending. Militant's position is thereby reinforced.

The one Liverpool local party that did not fall under the Braddock machine was Walton. There, according to one historian:

> The handful of Trotskyites had controlled the party for a while and had achieved the status almost of an 'establishment' of their own with 'fellow-travellers'—people who were left-wing but not 'Trotskyite', who wanted to keep the left wing as united as possible and were not particular about the company they kept. . . . In some respects Walton represented the fortress of the left wing—it was impregnable and unconcerned with anything outside its boundaries.[7]

It is in Walton that the first seeds of Militant can be identified, and in the 1950s the constituency secretary nurtured a group of young Trotskyists. At one point Walton chose Ted Grant as its candidate to fight the 1959 election, but the NEC refused to accept him. Later Peter Taaffe was a member of Walton Young Socialists.

Today Trotskyists are still strong in Walton. The party has been a frequent embarrassment for its left-wing MP, Eric Heffer. When Tony Benn challenged Denis Healey for Labour's deputy leadership in 1981 Heffer had wanted to stand too. But his local party said no. Heffer still finds his constituency party a problem from time to time.

In March 1958 the Walton party's youth magazine, *Rally*, fell into the hands of a young boilermaker called Terry Harrison. Harrison came from a lower-middle-class family and had originally joined the young Conservatives but had left them after Suez. He liked *Rally*'s Marxism and started going to meetings of the Walton youth section—the only active one in the city—even though he lived in Kirkdale. He began to read Trotsky. He also met other Marxists, among them future Executive members Pat Wall (then known as Paddy), Keith Dickinson and Peter Taaffe.

Taaffe did not arrive in Walton until two years later, in 1960, even though he had lived 'across the water' in Birkenhead. When doing his National Service, Harrison received from a friend back at home a letter about Taaffe, in which the future editor of *Militant* was described as a 'young lad' with 'promising ideas'.[8]

Peter Taaffe and Keith Dickinson eventually went to London to work full-time for Militant; Pat Wall moved away because of his job; but Harrison stayed behind looking after the home patch. Until ten years ago he worked as a boilermaker with Cammell Laird in Birkenhead but in 1973 put down his tools to become a full-timer. In the 1979 European elections Harrison stood for Labour in Liverpool, lost the seat and recorded an 11 per cent swing to the Tories, the highest in the country.

Harrison describes himself as a freelance journalist and insists that he no longer works full-time for Militant. He may not actually receive a salary from the tendency, but he is in effect the leader and father figure of Militant on Merseyside—local members call him 'Grandad'. At one time Harrison was on the Militant Editorial Board but now sits only on the Central Committee.

Jack Braddock was succeeded as Labour group leader by Alderman William Sefton, once Braddock's strongest critic in the Labour group. Just as in 1950 the left-wing Braddock had taken over a machine he once opposed, so now to a lesser extent did Sefton.

The 1960s saw Labour and Conservatives alternating in office on the Council, pursuing a largely bipartisan policy for the city. But at the end of the decade the Liberals suddenly emerged almost from nothing. The brilliant campaigning skills of a local businessman, Trevor Jones, exploited the growing disillusionment with the traditional parties. The term 'community politics' was introduced into Britain. 'Jones the Vote' was remarkably successful: the Liberals, who had just one councillor in 1967, became the largest single party after the 1973 elections.

For the next ten years no single party had a firm majority on the Council. Usually the Liberals held office but had to rely on Conservative support to hold power. Ian Craig, political editor of the *Liverpool Daily Post*, thinks that this three-party system, combined with Labour's frequent inability or refusal to take office, forced the Labour Party leftwards.[9] The party in opposition adopted policies that it might have abandoned long ago had it been in power, and the leadership no longer had the spoils of office with which to keep a grip on the party. Above all, there was an important shift in power from the Labour Group to the District Labour Party outside.

Most observers see 1972 as the year that really marked the end of the right's dominance of the Liverpool Labour Party. In the local elections that year the party in Liverpool had fought on a platform of outright opposition to any increase in

149

rents which might be caused by the Heath Government's Housing Finance Act. Within weeks of polling day, however, Sefton had abandoned this position. But he could get the required rent increases through Council only with support from the Conservatives and Liberals. Twenty-one Labour councillors voted against Sefton; they then broke away and formed a separate Labour group on the Council. What was important was that they won the backing of the Labour Party outside, and the Labour left resolved to make the Council leadership more accountable in future. Their task was made easier when Sefton lost his Council seat in the Liberal landslide the following year.

The early 1970s also saw among local Labour parties the first signs of discontent with their right-wing MPs. Richard Crawshaw in Toxteth, Sir Arthur Irvine in Edge Hill and Eric Ogden in West Derby all had problems.

In Toxteth Richard Crawshaw, an MP of great integrity, had met opposition ever since his first selection in 1962. In 1965 he had been 'nearly crucified' for voting against the Labour Government on the defence estimates—an act which would normally impress a local party but not in Crawshaw's case, since he was protesting that not enough money was going to the Territorial Army. In 1971 he voted with the Heath Government, and against the Labour whip, in the famous vote on entry to the EEC. Two years later he had to explain to his constituency executive why he had sponsored Dick Taverne when the rebel MP returned to the Commons after defeating Labour in the Lincoln by-election.

Eric Ogden's relations with his party were a bit better, but in 1975 he was censured for supporting a pay rise for MPs just at the time when the Labour Government was introducing another incomes policy.

The MP with the biggest problems, though, was Sir Arthur Irvine, Member for Edge Hill since 1947. Irvine was attacked for spending too much time on his London law practice and too little in his constituency. He visited Edge Hill once a month for surgeries, staying overnight at the Adelphi Hotel—for many years a class symbol in Liverpool (even though it was publicly owned until recently). Irvine's party was the most decrepit of all. Twice—in 1971 and 1972—it voted not to readopt Sir Arthur as its candidate. Somehow the MP got the decisions overturned on technical irregularities and survived to fight both elections in 1974.

In 1977 the party finally succeeded in ousting Irvine, by thirty-seven votes to three. The voting figures indicated not only Irvine's unpopularity but also how small his party was. The following year Sir Arthur died suddenly: his family blamed his death on the local party. The subsequent by-election was won by David Alton for the Liberals in a remarkable result. At the general election five weeks later Alton won again.

Sir Arthur blamed his downfall on what he saw as a 'Trotskyist–Liberal alliance'. That Irvine believed Trotsky-ists and Liberals might work together was a sign of how out of touch he was. In any case the Trotskyist strength in Edge Hill at that time was fairly limited, and the same was true in the other seats where MPs were having trouble. All three con-stituencies had in key positions Militant supporters who were naturally among each MP's sternest critics, but in every case dissatisfaction with the MP was also felt by a much wider group of people on the left and, in Irvine's case, by many on the right too.

When, after the 1979 general election, Crawshaw, Ogden and Dunn defected to the SDP one by one and were replaced by left-wingers it was not because Militant had been plotting their downfall, however delighted Militant was to see them go. The MPs had long been out of touch with their parties; they were no longer prepared to keep fighting. The reselec-tion system introduced in 1980 meant they would probably not survive, and with the advent of the SDP in 1981 they left the Labour Party. But for Militant the departures offered just the opportunity it wanted; within a year Militant candidates had been installed in four of Liverpool's eight seats; three of those seats had traditionally been Labour.

Most people say that it was in about 1978 or 1979 that Militant became a serious political force in Liverpool. A few Militant members had served on the Council before, but in those two years a block of seven was elected. This small triumph for Militant coincided with the last dying gasp of the right-wing old guard.

Since Sefton's departure in 1973 the Labour group had been led by John Hamilton, a quiet, modest left-winger who was a complete contrast to Braddock and Sefton. Hamilton had a long record of party service and was very popular, though regarded as rather weak: indeed, these two character-istics originally ensured his election. But in 1978, at the first meeting after the local elections, Hamilton was unexpectedly deposed in a coup by a Catholic right-winger, Eddie Roderick.

Within hours the local parties were in uproar. Wards and constituencies began to condemn the takeover and called for a new election. A special meeting of the district party was convened—with the highest attendance in years: after a stormy debate Roderick was forced to resign. In the new election several councillors switched their votes and Hamilton got his job back. He has held on to it ever since.

Roderick believes that Militant was largely responsible for the campaign that overturned his election and says that it was behind the resolutions passed by local parties and unions. At the special district party meeting he claims that councillors were warned by Militant speakers that if they did not vote the right way, they would be dropped as Council candidates.[10]

Roderick concedes, however, that Militant could not have succeeded without the support of the rest of the Liverpool left and of people who were genuinely outraged by what had happened. But whatever interpretation one puts on it, the incident illustrated the important shift in power which had occurred since the 1972 split. Braddock and Sefton had always been able to outmanoeuvre the district party, but now the Council leadership could no longer do so. The district party had become the more powerful of the two bodies. In particular it had learned how to use its power to draw up the list of approved candidates for Council elections. Several long-serving right-wing councillors had their careers brought to an abrupt halt through being dropped by the district party, though Roderick himself has survived.

It is on the District Labour Party General Committee that Militant has always been strongest in Liverpool, and it has used its position to exert influence elsewhere. Militant has never had a majority among the district party's elected delegates, but this has rarely mattered. Many of the union delegates never turn up. Militant supporters are always very diligent about attending meetings, and since it is extremely rare for even half the total delegates to turn up to district party meetings, they always have an effective majority. On the District Labour Party Executive Militant is even stronger; generally about half the members openly declare themselves supporters of the tendency.

The 1982 Council elections were the first occasion on which Labour had stood on an outright Militant platform with the slogan 'No Cuts in Jobs or Services, No Increases in Rents and No Increases in Rates'. It was a policy which the local party accepted would lead to 'clear confrontation with Mrs Thatcher's Government' if Labour won power. The district party's policy document stated:

> The entire strategy of the District Labour Party is based on the premise that the Council position should be used as a platform to expose the political bankruptcy of capitalism, educate the working class and provide a political

153

leadership on a local level to ensure a fight back against the Tory policy of cuts in public expenditure.[11]

Ted Grant could not have put it better himself. In the 1982 election campaign the Liberals exploited the 'Labour extremist' card to the full: posters went up saying 'Marxists Out, Liberals In'. But this propaganda did not seem to work, and Labour gained two seats. The following year the Liberals played down the anti-Militant line, but few voters in Liverpool can have been unaware by then that Militant had a strong position in the local Labour Party. It did not seem to worry them: Labour achieved an outstanding result in 1983, winning twenty-three of the thirty-three seats contested.

Militant supporters now hold many of the leading positions in the ruling Labour group. Most notable of their men is Derek Hatton, elected deputy leader in the summer of 1983. Young and charismatic, Hatton is clearly ambitious and is expert at handling the press. He always dresses smartly and often has a handkerchief poking out of his top pocket. It will not be long before Hatton succeeds John Hamilton, who is well beyond retirement age. Hatton's election as deputy leader was a sign of the respect he has earned in the Labour group for his hard work and enthusiasm. In the period since his election Hatton has effectively assumed the position of group leader. John Hamilton is rarely heard of: Hatton has been getting all the publicity in Liverpool's fight with the Government. His style of politics has even been compared with the boss politics of Jack Braddock.

Remarkably, perhaps, of the fifty-one councillors in the Labour group only about nine are actually members of Militant. But with the district party under their control, the tendency exerts much more influence than its numbers would lead one to expect. This is due to brilliant organization, as Eddie Roderick explained even before Labour took office:

All political parties, on the Monday before the Council meeting on a Wednesday, have a caucus meeting to decide the line of approach at the Council. The agenda for the meeting comes out on a Friday. The ten or twelve Militant members [a slight exaggeration] meet on either the Friday or the Saturday and go through the agenda to look for important policy decisions and for important vacancies. They then have a meeting with the broad left of the Labour group [an alliance of all the left-wing councillors] on Sunday morning at Pirrie Labour Club.... those Militants turn up in their full strength. There are generally about twenty people and the ten or eleven Militants there. They carry the majority vote there that commits the broad left for the meeting of the Labour group. On the Monday night at the Labour group of forty-two members the commitment that Militant have made themselves, plus other people they've taken along at the meeting on the Sunday morning, gives them a majority.... so you find that of forty-two Labour councillors, ten Militants control the policy of the Labour group.[12]

Roderick's analysis may be a rather simplified version of what happens, but his opponents do not substantially refute it. Militant councillors admit that they do get together to discuss forthcoming issues, but caucuses are not new to Liverpool Council. Until recently the Catholic Action group of Labour councillors met regularly. In Braddock's day there were three caucuses in all: Catholic Action, Braddock and his close allies—and the left, which has carried on meeting ever since. Caucusing like this is happening more and more in local government Labour groups: two of the best examples are Manchester Council and the Greater London Council. And, of course, at Westminster caucuses like the Tribune Group have been meeting for years.

The 'caucus-within-a-caucus' operation is also used by

Militant in Liverpool's local Labour parties and trade unions. According to Terry McDonald, former chairman of the Liverpool Kirkdale party, Militant members of the Management Committee would agree a line at their meeting, then persuade the Kirkdale broad left to accept it and finally use the broad left majority to win over the General Management Committee itself. It is exactly the method advocated by Trotsky in the 1930s with regard to the Independent Labour Party working within the Labour Party. Essentially it depends on members of each caucus sticking to the agreed line. In the Labour movement there is a long tradition of members of a group voting with a decided position, even if they disagree with it; hence the system of union block votes. But this kind of caucusing means that a minority within a body can be transformed into what is in effect a majority. For Militant the distinction is between 'physical' and 'political' control. 'Physical' control means having an absolute majority; 'political' control means being able to exert effective control, through good organization and caucusing, without an absolute majority. So long as non-Militant members of the broad left in Liverpool are prepared to carry on abiding by the caucus majority decisions, Militant will continue to exert 'political' control.

Eddie Roderick pays tribute to Militant's good organization and accepts that the record of Militant councillors' attendance at meetings is as good as his own. Roderick's problem is that right-wingers are not as conscientious. In what are often still very small parties the absence of one or two individuals can frequently make the difference between failure and success. But Militant does not try simply to ensure a good turn-out. Its caucus meetings will decide who is to propose, second and speak on motions, which amendments are to be accepted or rejected and even which points should be made at particular moments in the debate.

Militant's organization is better developed on Merseyside than anywhere else in the country and is co-ordinated by Terry Harrison. Militant refuses to say how many full-time workers it employs, fearing that the information might be used against it, but there appear to be at least six, possibly more. The only local employee whom Militant will identify is Richard Venton, its official Merseyside spokesman, who was born and brought up in Northern Ireland but never became involved in Ulster politics. He joined Militant and the Labour Party on his arrival at Liverpool University in 1972. After his studies he spent a short time teaching before becoming a Militant employee four years ago.

Apart from Terry Harrison and Richard Venton, the other key Militant figure is Tony Aitman. Aitman actually denies he works full-time for the organization; like Harrison, he says he is a freelance journalist. Recently he claimed to have sent articles to the *Daily Express*, the *Daily Mirror*, *The Times* and the *Economist*.[13] But Aitman admits that he has not been very successful in his journalistic career: these journals have never heard of him and, when pressed, Aitman admits that he has had articles published only in *Militant*. Unlike Terry Harrison, he is not a member of the journalists' union, the NUJ: he says that since he has had nothing published, it would be 'pointless' to join.[14] Aitman's position is particularly odd, since many of Militant's full-time journalists, as opposed to organizers, are NUJ members.

Militant's official Merseyside headquarters is at 2 Lower Breck Road, Kirkdale, a semi-detached house that Militant bought from the local Labour Party in 1980 for £9,000. Like those of other Militant buildings, the windows are covered by iron grilles and the door in sheet metal. A large room on the ground floor is let to local Labour parties and other groups for meetings and election work, but no one except members of Militant is ever allowed into the rooms on the top floor.

As well as work in the Labour Party, Militant is becoming heavily involved in Merseyside trade unions and with broad left groups in many local union branches. A Merseyside Militant supporter, Phil Holt, is convener of a committee which co-ordinates the work of broad left groups at national level. In June 1983 Holt was one of three Militant supporters elected to the Executive of the Post Office Engineering Union in a shift to the left at the union's conference. In the past the Merseyside trade union movement was dominated by the manual unions, which were run by the Communist Party. With economic decline these unions have lost their strength and have been replaced by the new white-collar unions. The shift in power from blue-collar to white-collar unions which has occurred at national level and is reflected by the composition of the TUC General Council, has been particularly pronounced in Liverpool. The docks and industry have been replaced as sources of employment by the public sector. On Merseyside this shift has seen a transfer of influence from the Communist Party to Militant. Militant is particularly strong in the local government union, NALGO, the Civil Service union, CPSA, and the Post Office Engineering Union. At the same time the tendency has also built itself up in the Transport and General Workers' Union, once the stronghold of the Communist Party.

Militant is by no means as strong in the local unions as it is in the Labour Party, however, and many people feel that if the tendency is to be dislodged in Liverpool, that could be achieved through a concerted effort within the union movement. Many of the unions where Militant is strong are not affiliated to the party anyway. Union delegates actually hold a majority of places in the District Labour Party, but many of the delegates never turn up. If they did, Militant could be beaten. But who would replace them? Until a few years ago the right-wing old guard was the only alternative to Militant, but in recent months a left-wing group has slowly emerged within the Liverpool party that in time could pose a serious threat to Militant on the Council and in the constituencies.

This new force is organized around the Merseyside Labour Co-ordinating Committee and *Merseyside Labour Briefing:* both can be described as 'non-Militant left'. The Merseyside Labour Co-ordinating Committee is a local branch of the policy pressure group which was set up by supporters of Tony Benn in 1978 but has since drifted away from Benn. *Briefing* is one of a number of provincial versions of *London Labour Briefing,* the magazine set up by Ken Livingstone and several of his colleagues on the Greater London Council and in London politics. Many in the two Merseyside groups are quite new to the party, coming from the women's movement, the Communist Party or smaller left-wing bodies like the International Marxist Group. They are mainly university-educated, middle-class, professional types—a contrast to the largely working-class membership of Militant. The groups reflect the new generation of left-wing activists associated with Ken Livingstone, Tony Benn and the 'hard left' who have made so much of the running in the Labour Party in recent years.

These groups are not yet trying to counter Militant organizationally: there is no attempt to beat Militant candidates in internal party elections. The groups are not strong enough for this yet but, more important, they do not believe in the rigid discipline and tactics of Militant's democratic centralism: in many cases this is just the style of politics that prompted them to leave other groups and join the Labour Party. Nor did the new Liverpool left support the leadership's campaign against Militant.

The Co-ordinating Committee and *Briefing* have concentrated their efforts on local party policy. In recent months they have opposed Militant over the previous Liberal

Council's plans for positive discrimination for blacks, which Militant said would divide working-class people. They have also proposed alternative policies for education and, in particular, have rejected Militant's opposition to housing co-operatives, which were successfully pioneered by the previous Liberal Council. Militant's line, 'No Cuts in Jobs or Services, No Increases in Rents and No Increases in Rates', has been attacked as unrealistic. So far the Liverpool 'new left' has not had much success, but the policy work has provided a focal point for opponents of Militant and has forced Militant to justify its policies on many issues. Formerly Militant's proposals often went through on the nod because there was no alternative.

Militant cannot be blamed for seizing the opportunity presented to it in Liverpool:

> A political vacuum opened up in the Labour Party—to be filled, in the absence of anything more coherent, by Young Socialists equipped with the strident, urgent politics of Militant. Following meekly behind, a mere handful of the intuitively left old guard, unable to think of anything better. The Militant is heard as Labour's voice because it is the only voice to be heard. ... Sectarian to a fault, its main activity is making platform speeches and waging warfare within the Labour ranks. Its practice, despite the noise, is traditional and remarkably similar to that of the right-wing old guard.[15]

That right-wing old guard, or what remains of it, has only itself to blame for its present predicament, for allowing Militant to become so strong. Jack Braddock and his colleagues developed a machine style of politics in Liverpool which readily suited Militant. At the same time the old regime initiated policies which came to be rejected by both the party and its voters, which all worked to Militant's long-term advantage. But on top of that Braddock had deliberately weakened his own party at the organizational level, and this provided just the opportunity that this small, dedicated group needed.

Under Militant's influence the new ruling Labour group has reversed the redundancies previously planned by the Liberals, has resumed the filling of job vacancies and has started creating 1,000 new jobs. Council house rents have been cut by £2 a week, and the Council is likely to be at least £90 million in deficit in the year 1984–5. Labour councillors have been rallying the Council unions in readiness for a major confrontation with Whitehall, and there is the possibility that the Government will send commissioners in to run the city. There was even talk of the Government scrapping the May 1984 Council elections, while many other Labour councils were urging Liverpool to join a concerted campaign against the Government and not to 'go it alone'. If the Council wins the battle, Militant will undoubtedly claim it as a 'victory for socialist ideas'. If it capitulates in the face of severe financial and political pressures, as several other Labour councils have done in the past, one can be sure that the minority of Militant councillors within the Labour group will not have voted for the compromise. No, they will be able to denounce the action of their Labour colleagues as yet another in the long history of 'betrayals' by leaders of the working class.

10

Foot Steps Forward

For the Labour leadership the 'winter of discontent' of 1979 turned into a summer that was far from glorious and an autumn that was a disaster. Labour's defeat at the polls in May that year unleashed all the dissatisfaction which had been building up among party activists over the past five years. Jim Callaghan was not only blamed for getting the date of the election wrong but was also held responsible for the confrontation with the unions during the previous winter which had lost Labour millions of votes. The start of the 1979 election campaign had seen a row over whether the abolition of the House of Lords should be included in the manifesto. For the left Callaghan's insistence that the policy be excluded typified everything that was wrong with the party and only strengthened the belief that constitutional reforms were badly needed.

The 1979 Conference in Brighton saw a major defeat for the right. Delegate after delegate laid into the party leadership, and the assembly agreed, at least in principle, to two important constitutional changes that the left had been demanding for years: mandatory reselection of MPs, and the NEC's sole responsibility for drawing up the election manifesto. Brighton 1979 also marked the start of four years of internal wrangling which eventually helped to deny the Labour Party victory in 1983. Militant was just one of several important issues which would divide left from right.

Two months after the 1979 election the National Agent, Reg Underhill, retired, having served the party all his working life. His reward was a seat in the Lords. Underhill was looking forward to a rest from party organizational matters; he hoped to concentrate on being an Opposition spokesman in the upper chamber. But before long he came under intense pressure from right-wing MPs and journalists to make public the work on Militant which the Labour NEC had refused to publish when he was a party official. Underhill eventually decided to update his Militant report with new evidence that he had received. In January 1980 he sent his new report to the General Secretary, Ron Hayward, and to his successor as National Agent, David Hughes. But Hughes was not interested in Militant. He did not even bother to read the report. 'We dealt with it and that was the end of it,' he is reported to have remarked. 'I have a lot of other things to do. This job carries a heavy work load. We *have* just lost an election, you know.'[1]

A right-wing Labour MP, Neville Sandelson, who was battling against the left in his Hayes and Harlington constituency party (only some of whom were Militant members), formally asked the NEC to consider the new Underhill report and to publish it. Meanwhile Underhill made it known that if the NEC did not make the report public, he might go ahead and publish it himself.

Not surprisingly, the revival of the Militant issue rekindled press interest. Sandelson and other right-wing Labour MPs were only too happy to keep journalists informed. The *Daily Mirror* managed to get hold of a copy of Underhill's report and made a front-page story of it.[2] The *Sunday Times* printed an article on Militant's finances, asking where a loan of £148,000 had come from.[3] Both *New Society*[4] and the *New Statesman*[5] published long and well researched articles on Militant, and the new BBC 2 programme *Newsnight* showed a film report which was based partly on Charles James's work on Militant's finances.[6] This also included a dramatic interview with a Militant defector called 'Jane', filmed in the back of a car travelling through the streets of London.

When the NEC met in February it decided that the best thing to do was to send a questionnaire to all the pressure groups operating within the party, including Militant, asking for details about their organization, finances and democratic procedures. But the NEC decided not to set up what it called an 'inquisition' or to publish Underhill's work. Its resolution concluded: 'The National Executive Committee invites Lord Underhill to publish any documents he wishes to publish.'[7] So he did.

> I said to my wife, 'How much can we afford?' [Underhill recalls] and then we printed 750 copies at our own expense. I had built up a list of addresses of constituency secretaries, and my daughter typed out the labels and filled the envelopes. We sent a copy to each NEC member, each constituency party and every affiliated trade union.[8]

Further copies of the twenty-nine page report were sold to journalists to help meet printing and postage costs, and with several donations from individuals Lord Underhill ended up only about £70 out of pocket on a venture which had originally cost approximately £700. As might be expected, the release of the report received further wide coverage in the press, and several papers printed long extracts. But it was clear that the NEC was not going to take any further action.

The left, which was still in control of the NEC, had no wish to attack Militant, and it increasingly needed the tendency's support in the important battles over democratizing the party. Tony Benn told a television interviewer: 'I remember the Zinoviev letter was a forgery', and he dismissed the Underhill documents. 'As far as I can make out [they] came in plain envelopes from the Intelligence Service or wherever.' Eric Heffer compared the new campaign against Militant with Goebbels' Nazi propaganda.[9]

Significantly, the increasingly influential Campaign for Labour Party Democracy welcomed the NEC decision not to publish Underhill's evidence. In May 1980 several left-wing groups got together to form the new Rank and File Mobilizing Committee (RFMC), designed to unite the left in the battle for democratic reforms. The feeling was that success had been impeded in the past by lack of co-ordination. Militant was invited to send two delegates, and the Labour Party Young Socialists, controlled by Militant, also had two people on the Committee. For the first time Militant had agreed to involve itself in a grouping which was outside its control—a sign of just how important Militant considered the constitutional proposals. As it turned out, Militant was to play only a minor role in the RFMC itself: according to one account, its delegates rarely attended the meetings, and it never contributed money or distributed RFMC bulletins.[10] But the important point is that Militant did abide by its decisions. The RFMC could later claim much of the credit for the two important constitutional changes finally agreed in 1980: mandatory reselection of MPs, and the election of the party leader by a new electoral college comprising MPs, unions and constituency parties. (NEC control of the manifesto, agreed in principle in 1979, was defeated in 1980.)

A few days after the 1980 Conference Jim Callaghan resigned as leader, and Michael Foot was elected to succeed him (under the old system of election by MPs—the exact composition of the new electoral college had not yet been decided). Foot is reported to have been shocked by his victory. The cause was partly surprise that he had won (Denis Healey was the favourite) but probably more a sudden realization of the responsibilities thrust upon him. As the 'unity' candidate, Foot was now expected to hold together a party in which civil war had been waging for several months.

Michael Foot's first year as leader must have turned out to be a bigger nightmare than even he had feared. Within weeks of his election came the special conference at Wembley to agree the precise make-up of the electoral college. Contrary to expectations, this gave the unions the biggest share—40 per cent of the votes, against 30 per cent each for the MPs and the constituencies. A right-wing union, USDAW, had unexpectedly put forward the 40–30–30 formula after Militant supporters had lobbied several members of the union's delegation. The day after Wembley, a Sunday, came the Limehouse Declaration and, a few weeks later, the formation of the Social Democratic Party. Foot had pleaded with the Social Democrats to stay but with no success. Then almost as soon as that problem had subsided there came another. Tony Benn suddenly announced, early one morning in April, that he was going to test the new electoral college by challenging Denis Healey for the deputy leadership.

The deputy leadership of the Labour Party is an odd post. Like the Vice-Presidency of the United States, it confers more prestige than power. Deputy leaders rarely proceed to greater glory: Foot is the only one since Attlee to become leader. Perhaps its only advantage is that the job gives the incumbent an automatic place on the NEC and in the Shadow Cabinet. But, for some peculiar reason, in the summer of 1981 the post of Labour Party Deputy Leader suddenly assumed a new significance, especially when, as the Conference drew near, it looked as if Benn might win. Arguably, the election received wider media publicity than the leadership battle of 1983.[11]

Party activists thought the contest vitally important too. Those bodies which had campaigned vigorously for constitutional changes now pulled out all the stops for Benn. Militant was among them. But the campaign also marked the begin-

ning of a significant rift on the left: Tribunites Neil Kinnock
and Joan Lestor were never forgiven by the Bennites for
abstaining. And throughout the six-month campaign Michael
Foot made it clear that he was furious with Benn for standing
in the first place. In the end Denis Healey held on ('by a
whisker' was the common description). And then, almost
every day of the SDP Conference the following week, came
news of another right-wing MP's defection to the SDP.
Nearly every one of them had cast their votes for Healey the
week before.

This period also saw the first signs that trade union leaders
were becoming worried about Militant. Until the late 1970s
Militant had concentrated its work on the Labour Party and
had made little impact on the unions. After the establishment
of its Industrial Bureau in the mid-1970s, Militant saw its
work in the unions as the natural extension to its work in the
Labour Party. It was regarded as another means of raising
workers' consciousness and finding new recruits. Where the
unions were affiliated to the Labour Party, it could be a new
source of voting power at party meetings. By the start of the
1980s the tendency was having small but increasing success
in this field. Progress had often been helped by unsuccessful
industrial action. The 1977–8 firemen's strike, for instance,
prompted Militant gains in the Fire Brigades' Union, and the
1980 steel strike increased Militant's influence in the Iron
and Steel Trades' Confederation. In 1979, after the unsuccessful 1978 bakers' strike, a Militant member, Joe Marino,
was elected General Secretary of the Bakers' Union. Above
all Militant had been gaining ground in the Civil Service
unions, in particular the CPSA, where Militant had been progressing since the mid-1970s. Eventually, in 1982, after the
long and unsuccessful Civil Service strike, the union elected a
Militant member, Kevin Roddy, as president, though he was
deposed after a year.

As it had in many local Labour parties, Militant often

made progress in unions through its work in the new broad left groups. Militant is usually a minority within these left-wing alliances, but, as in Liverpool, clever organization can give it disproportionate influence. In the CPSA Militant's strength within one major branch, the DHSS branch in Newcastle, helped it to achieve almost a majority on the union's Executive. Militant had also made progress within two other white-collar unions, the Society of Civil and Public Servants and the local government union NALGO, (although, like CPSA, these unions are not affiliated to the Labour Party), and it had had small successes in the miners' union, the Transport and General Workers' Union, the shop-workers' union (USDAW), the Post Office engineers' union and the railwaymen's union (the NUR).

In the past calls for action against Militant had come almost entirely from MPs and party officials, but after the 1979 election right-wing unions became increasingly concerned about the tendency too. The clerical workers' union, APEX, called for action after the 1980 Underhill report, and later in the year the NUR annual conference called on the Labour Party to bring back the Proscribed List. They sent a similar resolution to the 1981 Labour Conference, but there was not enough support to secure a debate. The resolution was remitted (passed to the NEC for consideration).

After the 1981 Brighton Conference Michael Foot was coming under increasing pressure from the right. The implied threat was that if he did not act against the far left, the ranks of Labour MPs would shrink still further. Throughout the autumn of 1981 a steady flow of MPs trickled from Labour to the Social Democrats. The possibility of further departures, perhaps on a large scale, was a constant worry for Foot, especially at a time when Labour was falling behind the Liberals and the SDP in the polls and in by-elections. In October the right-wing Manifesto Group of MPs went to see Foot about something else that had been troubling them for some months: the selection of Militant members as Labour parliamentary candidates.

Several years earlier Militant had spoken internally of 'establishing a group of half a dozen or so MPs identified with the tendency',[12] but until now little progress had been made towards this aim. This plan was not part of some long-term scheme eventually to take over the Parliamentary Labour Party: the thinking was simply that candidates and MPs would give Militant a powerful platform from which more people could be won over to the ideas of the tendency. In 1979 three Militant candidates had stood for Labour: Tony Mulhearn in Crosby, David White in Croydon Central and Cathy Wilson on the Isle of Wight. But only White, in a marginal seat, got much publicity. All three candidates lost with slightly larger than average swings against them (see Appendix 2).

But in 1980 and 1981 the tendency began to get more candidates selected and this time in good seats. It almost looked as if a deliberate decision had suddenly been taken by Militant to go for safe seats: in reality the tendency was simply being more successful. By October 1981 five Militant members had been chosen; three of them were in Labour seats (Pat Wall in Bradford North, Tony Mulhearn in Liverpool Toxteth and David Nellist in Coventry South-East). Two more were in former Labour seats which the party could hope to regain in a good year (Terry Harrison in Liverpool Edge Hill and Rod Fitch in Brighton Kemptown). And the word was that a sixth Militant candidate would soon be chosen in another safe seat, Liverpool Kirkdale. To the right it seemed as if Militant was now reaping the benefits of the re-selection process for which it had helped to fight. To some extent that was true. As we have seen, in two Liverpool seats with Militant candidates (Toxteth and Kirkdale) right-wing MPs defected to the SDP knowing that they would probably not be reselected by their parties, which had a strong Militant presence. But the case that worried the right most was Bradford North.

There, in October 1981, one of the founders of Militant, Pat Wall, had defeated the sitting MP, Ben Ford, by thirty-five votes to twenty-eight. Ford was well to the right of the party and had made himself unpopular by visiting countries with right-wing dictatorships. Wall, on the other hand, was a popular figure in the area, having been president of Bradford Trades Council since 1973. At the age of 16, in 1950, Wall had been party secretary in Liverpool Garston and was their Conference delegate the following year. His work for *Rally*, *Socialist Fight* and *Militant* over the years had accompanied long service to the labour movement. Wall had been a councillor in both Liverpool and Bingley and had become a familiar figure at Labour conferences, usually managing to speak at least once whenever he was a delegate. Since 1973 he had been a regular candidate for the Labour NEC (see Appendix 1) and had more than once got the highest vote of any non-MP.

Wall has the lifestyle of a man from a working-class background who has done well in life. Earning more than £15,000 a year as a hardware buyer with a mail-order firm, he owns a small cottage on the edge of the moors. He is different from most of the other Militant founder members, more of an individual. He declines to serve on the Militant Central Committee because he does not have the time. Though clearly committed to Militant, politics are not the only thing in his life: he likes listening to jazz and goes clay-pigeon shooting. Most Saturdays he travels around the country to support Everton Football Club.

The Bradford North constituency had had a weak party, with only about 150 members, in the mid-1970s. Militant had taken advantage of this weakness and had become a strong force in the constituency, but when Wall was chosen it was by no means in a majority. In other places Militant candidates had been selected simply because the tendency had taken control of a party (as in some of the Liverpool seats), but this was not the case in Bradford North. Wall got the nomination because of two extra ingredients, personal popularity and his party record, not simply because he was a member of Militant.

But the right-wing Manifesto Group were not the only MPs calling on Foot to take action in the autumn of 1981. At Westminster several groups were regularly meeting together to discuss their grievances and then present them to Foot. One of these was the Group of Ten. They were all young Turks—mostly MPs in their late thirties or early forties who could expect to be promoted to ministerial positions in a future Labour Government. Their growing fear was that they might be old men before there was such a Government again. The group comprised five right-wingers (Phillip Whitehead, Ken Woolmer, John Cunningham, Ann Taylor and Giles Radice) and five members of the Tribune Group (Jack Straw, Jeff Rooker, Arthur Davidson, Robert Kilroy-Silk and Andrew Bennett). The ten met for lunches and dinners at each other's London homes and were to carry on meeting right up to the 1983 election. Later they would make efforts to remove Foot as leader, but at this point, in the autumn of 1981, their sole aim was to persuade the Labour leader to change course. More than once delegations from the Group of Ten went to see Foot.

This period really marks the turning-point in relations between Militant and the party establishment. The key figure was Michael Foot. Until then he had helped to prevent any action against Militant, but afterwards he was to the fore in initiating it.

The crucial incident that changed Foot's conciliatory attitude to the far left occurred at the beginning of November 1981. In a Commons debate on the privatization of North Sea oil Tony Benn announced from his position on the front bench that when Labour got back into power it would take the assets back 'without compensation'. This was not Shadow Cabinet policy. Benn could possibly argue that it was Conference policy, but for Foot that was no excuse. The Labour leader was furious and let it be known that he did not want Benn re-elected to the Shadow Cabinet. Only weeks before he had been asking Benn to stand again. MPs duly followed their leader, and Benn was voted on to the back benches.

Foot is reported to have told one NEC meeting that since being elected leader he had received hundreds of letters from 'the people I marched with at Aldermaston' telling him to take action against the far left. At a Parliamentary Labour Party meeting he complained of 'caucusitis' and called Militant a 'pestilential nuisance'. Then, at the NEC Organization Committee, he supported a call for an inquiry to look into Militant's activities. But Militant was not the only victim of the new Michael Foot. His tough stand was also directed against a young, unknown left-winger called Peter Tatchell, who had just been selected as candidate for Bermondsey but not yet endorsed by the NEC. Warning only his closest colleagues, during Prime Minister's Questions Foot told the Commons that Tatchell would never be a Labour Party 'member' (he meant to say 'candidate'). Apparently the sitting MP, Bob Mellish, an old-style right-winger and former Chief Whip who was due to retire, had threatened that if Tatchell were endorsed as candidate, he would resign as the MP at once. That would have forced an embarrassing by-election, which the SDP might easily have won. But, perhaps crucially, on the day on which Foot made his Commons statement a member of the Group of Ten had shown him an article in *London Labour Briefing* in which Tatchell had written of the need for 'more militant forms of extra-parliamentary opposition which involve mass popular participation and challenge the Government's right to rule'.[13]

Having condemned Tatchell to the nation, Foot decided that he had now better rally the support of people on the NEC.

Fortunately for Foot, the NEC had swung rightwards at the 1981 Conference, but to ensure a majority Foot still needed the support of people who were now being called 'soft-left', notably Neil Kinnock and Joan Lestor. At the December 1981 NEC, with the soft left's support, Foot won the day as far as both Tatchell and Militant were concerned. But even people on the right thought that in Tatchell's case Foot had gone too far and that his denunciation of the young candidate was a great tactical error. They were also annoyed that Foot had not consulted anybody before condemning him. But there was little the right could do about it now. As leader, Foot had to be supported in his battle against the left, even if his tactics were wrong. Many members of the NEC— particularly some of the long-serving trade unionists—saw themselves as 'leadership loyalists' rather than 'moderates'. If Foot had proposed a day-trip to Mars, some NEC members would have gone with him. The left often described Michael Foot as the 'prisoner' of a right-wing NEC, but from this point onwards it was Foot who took much of the initiative in fighting the far left.

The NEC set up a full-scale inquiry to look into Militant. Compared with the investigations in 1977, it looked now as if the inquiry would result in strong action against the tendency, including expulsions.

For the next fifteen months the stories of Militant and Peter Tatchell were to merge, at least in the public mind. Several tabloid papers repeatedly described Tatchell as a member of Militant in spite of his continual denials.[14] Politically Tatchell's views are more in tune with the new left than with Militant, and for its part Militant dislikes not only Tatchell's 'community politics' but also the fact that he is gay. Tatchell has described recently how Militant members waged a 'word-of-mouth campaign' against him in Bermondsey and had never wanted him as candidate,[15] but these differences were not always apparent at the time. The confusion may also have had something to do with the fact that Peter Tatchell and Peter Taaffe have similar names. Another issue to be confused with these was that of Tariq Ali, the former leader of the International Marxist Group. Ali had decided that Labour was now where the future lay, had left the IMG and had applied to join the Hornsey Labour Party. Hornsey was happy to give Ali a membership card, but the NEC refused to accept him.

The two men asked to carry out the Militant investigation were Ron Hayward, the General Secretary, who was about to retire, and David Hughes, the National Agent. In view of their past attitude to such matters, neither man can have viewed the job with much relish.

Nevertheless Hayward and Hughes quickly set about their task. Regional Organizers were asked to send in reports on Militant activities in their areas. Most complied, though the Scottish organizer, James Allison, refused, saying he had no intention of becoming a 'private investigator'.[16] They also received a large amount of unsolicited material from MPs and ordinary party members. A lot of this 'evidence' was poor, along the lines of: 'And then he tried to sell me a copy of Militant . . . .' But there were many useful contributions. Labour Solidarity enlisted the help of Lord Underhill and the evidence of several defectors to compile a seventeen-page report detailing Militant's history, organization and finances; Roy Hattersley subedited it, adding a few literary touches. Another helpful contribution came from the party's Student Organizer, John Dennis, who had been approached by Hughes. Dennis rewrote one of Charles James's reports on the finances, provided an account from David Mason (see chapter 8) of his experiences in the tendency and gave details himself on how Militant operates within NOLS. One of several MPs to submit evidence was Frank Field, who

174

argued, among other things, that Militant should be asked to hand over its full-time workers, newspaper and printing network to the Labour Party.[17]

Hayward and Hughes also received information from Militant defectors, some of whom they interviewed. Militant too was approached. At the start of the inquiry it was sent a list of questions about the organization. In reply Peter Taaffe said that the Editorial Board consisted of five people: himself, Lynn Walsh, Ted Grant, Clare Doyle and Keith Dickinson and declared that there were sixty-four full-time staff. This statement was never really challenged. Towards the end of the investigation, in May, Hayward and Hughes interviewed Taaffe, Grant and Walsh at Walworth Road.

But while the Hayward–Hughes inquiry was progressing, there were important developments elsewhere. In January 1982 the NEC and several trade union leaders met at the ASTMS college at Bishop's Stortford to try to sort out some of the party's problems. The weekend ended with the declaration: 'Peace has broken out in the party.' What this meant in practice was not clear. Did it mean, for instance, that the inquiry into Militant would be dropped? Nobody was sure. Hayward and Hughes carried on with their work but, it seems, with less fervour than before. People who had earlier been encouraged to give evidence suddenly found that there was not much interest in their contributions.

Meanwhile the Pat Wall controversy dragged on. Ben Ford, MP for Bradford North, had made some rather petty allegations of irregularities in the selection procedure, and so a three-man NEC inquiry team had visited Bradford and recommended that a new selection be got underway. But the Organization Committee, no doubt feeling that it was upholding the 'spirit of Bishop's Stortford', rejected the inquiry's recommendation on the grounds that one member of the team, John Golding, had declared beforehand that Pat Wall should not be the candidate. Instead the committee

175

recommended that Wall's candidature be accepted. But the NEC, in turn, rejected the Org-Sub's report and called for a new selection. Then by coincidence, the day before the Organization Committee was due to meet yet again, the *Sunday Times* ran a front-page 'exclusive' story about Pat Wall under the headline 'New Shock for Foot—Labour Man Urges Overthrow of State'.[18]

The paper's political correspondent, Michael Jones, had gone to a meeting in Bradford at which Wall had been debating with the Socialist Workers' Party and secretly tape-recorded Wall's speech. Wall was recorded as saying the 'issue of Parliament' was a minor one, and that a Marxist Labour Government would have to deal with the capitalist state machine immediately on coming to office:

> It would mean the abolition of the monarchy, the House of Lords, the sacking of the generals, the admirals, the air marshals, the senior civil servants, the police chiefs and in particular, the judges and people of that character.... We will face bloodshed. We will face the possibility of civil war and the terrible death and destruction and bloodshed that would mean.[19]

The story was milked for all it was worth—and more. *Sunday Times* readers must have been appalled to discover, for instance, that the potential Labour candidate had spoken in a hall where 'jeans predominated among both sexes', and a baby 'dozed in a portable cot'.[20] Unfortunately for Wall, the *Sunday Times* story was not entirely just, and the follow-up by other papers was even less fair. Wall had not himself been advocating bloodshed but had said that violence would be a *reaction* to a Marxist Government's coming to power. The article said that Wall had 'shared the platform of the revolutionary Socialist Workers' Party', when really he was just taking part in a debate with it. But once again the facts of the case were overridden by the impression it created.

Jones's tape-recording was played on radio and television bulletins that Sunday. The *Daily Mail* and *Daily Telegraph* ran the story as their front-page leads the following day.[21] Newsmen flocked to Pat Wall's home in Bradford, where his wife Pauline retaliated by taking photos of the photographers and posting up a copy of the NUJ Code of Conduct.

The Hayward–Hughes inquiry reported in June, though its recommendations were leaked widely in advance of official publication. The three-page report contained nothing new and no evidence against Militant. It concluded that Militant was 'not a group formed solely to support a newspaper' and that the tendency was 'in conflict with Clause II, Section 3, of the party constitution'. The two officials recommended that the NEC should set up a register of non-affiliated groups of members which would be allowed to operate within the party. In their opinion, 'the Militant Tendency [sic] as presently constituted would not be eligible to be included on the proposed Register in the light of our findings.'[22]

It was a solution that satisfied hardly anybody. The right wanted to know why none of the evidence had been published and why Militant had to be dealt with in such a roundabout manner. It wanted definite expulsions, possibly through the reintroduction of the Proscribed List. The register seemed to pose all sorts of problems. It was not clear what would happen to Militant once the register was established. What would the party do if other groups refused to register, in sympathy with Militant? Would they be expelled too? And there was a general feeling that it was unfair to declare Militant excluded from the register before it had had a chance to apply. Peter Taaffe said that the register would inevitably lead to expulsions, though privately Militant believed that the number of names on the hit list was small. 'Hayward doesn't want to go down in history as a witch-hunter-general,' Taaffe said to one journalist on his return from the meeting with Hayward and Hughes. The far left said it was the beginning of a witch-hunt against the whole of the left, and a group called the Unregistered Alliance was formed. As the Labour Party's own paper, *Labour Weekly*, commented on the register: 'it could only work in an atmosphere of co-operation. There is no evidence that such an atmosphere exists.'[23]

The register proposal was thought up by Dick Clements, who had just been appointed an adviser to Michael Foot after twenty-one years as editor of *Tribune*. The idea of a register of party groups had previously been proposed by the left-wing Labour Co-ordinating Committee. But the Committee saw it as a means of assisting the large number of pressure groups within the party by providing them with official back-up from party headquarters (such as constituency secretaries' addresses); it did not see the register as a means of acting against groups.

The register was a typical Labour Party compromise, however. Hayward, Hughes and Foot all knew in the summer of 1982 that they would not necessarily win support for outright expulsions, either on the NEC or at the coming Conference. Michael Foot said the party would have been within its rights to expel Militant there and then but still argued, 'If there is some other way, we should seek a remedy.'[24] The register would almost certainly lead to some expulsions, of course, but at this stage they could not spell that out. Expulsions would be delayed until the register itself had been agreed by Conference and until a more favourable NEC had been elected, as seemed likely. It was also seen as a means of avoiding the revival of the notorious Proscribed List, which had been abolished in 1973. What was not realized at the time was just how much the procedure would delay the matter. It would be another eight months before any expulsions took place, and that period would see another of the long-drawn-out battles in which the Labour Party seems to specialize.

Meanwhile, two days after the Hayward–Hughes report was accepted by the NEC, Pat Wall was selected again by Bradford North. This time his majority over Ben Ford was much larger—forty-nine votes to twelve (compared with thirty-five to twenty-eight before). 'Now what the hell are they going to do?' Wall asked.[25] The same day Ron Hayward retired as General Secretary, to be succeeded by Jim Mortimer, former chairman of the conciliation service, ACAS, and once victim of the former Proscribed List.

Mortimer had played no role in the preparation of the Hayward–Hughes report, but it was now his job to make sure that the register worked and to carry out the disciplinary action. Mortimer had a long-standing dislike of Trotskyist groups. In his left-wing youth the new General Secretary had had links with orthodox Communists rather than with their Trotskyist enemies. Ironically Militant had grudgingly voted for Mortimer's appointment.

A notice was placed in *Labour Weekly* asking pressure groups to apply for registration. But some union leaders told Mortimer and Foot that they could not be sure of enlisting the support of their unions—some had already passed resolutions against expulsions and witch-hunts. The job would be much easier, some union leaders said, if the evidence against Militant had been published.

Over the summer the question of the register became an important issue on the left, almost a symbol of left-wing virility. Some organizations, such as the Tribune Group of MPs and the Labour Co-ordinating Committee, did register. Others, such as the Campaign for Labour Party Democracy and the Labour Abortion Rights Campaign, refused at first. Michael Foot staked his leadership on the register decision, but as unions held their summer conferences and meetings to decide on policy for the forthcoming Labour Party Conference in Blackpool, it was increasingly clear that even though most constituencies were against the register, the union block votes would probably save Foot from defeat.

At the beginning of September Militant held what they called a 'Labour Movement Conference' at Wembley. In effect it was a show of strength against the Labour leadership, as 2,600 Militant members and sympathizers came from all over the country to protest about the witch-hunt. The gathering received wide coverage in the press and on television. Earlier that summer Tony Benn had agreed to sponsor the occasion, but another engagement prevented him from attending, and he merely sent a message of support—a sign perhaps that the leader of the left wished to distance himself from the tendency. In fact, the only MP willing to attend was Les Huckfield, who was at that point in severe danger of losing both his place on the Labour NEC and his seat in Parliament (in the end he lost both). This was rather ironic, since Huckfield had a long history of vehement opposition to the tendency. In his youth Huckfield had campaigned against Trotskyists in the LPYS in the West Midlands. Much later, in 1978, when a junior Minister, Huckfield had gone to see John Golding at the Department of Employment with a list of people whom he believed to be Militant full-timers. He suggested that Golding might like to investigate whether any of them were also claiming state benefits.

The 1982 Labour Party Conference was a low-key affair compared with the three historic conferences that had preceded it. For most people in Blackpool the main interest of the week was whether the right would manage to strengthen its position on the NEC.

The Militant debate took place on the Monday afternoon, the first day of Conference. For the television companies and the press this was the big set piece of the week. Sitting in the gallery were the five public members of Militant's Editorial Board, all of whom must have thought that once the register was approved, it would be only a few weeks before they were expelled from the party.

The debate was opened by Jim Mortimer, who formally presented the Hayward-Hughes report on behalf of the NEC. It was his first speech to Conference as General Secretary. '. . . Militant is not just a newspaper. The Militant Tendency [sic] is an organized faction—an organized party—within the Labour Party,' Mortimer argued. 'It has, first, its own long-term programme, principles and policy—quite distinct from those of the Labour Party.'[26] Mortimer spoke of the huge 'trunk' of evidence accumulated at Walworth Road but did not give any details of it. But, perhaps surprisingly, nearly half of his address was devoted to attacking Militant's policies and ideology. He criticized its attitude to trade unionism and its treatment of wider popular groups such as the women's movement and the campaign against nuclear weapons. And he denounced Militant's approach to 'détente and the relaxation of international tension', calling Militant members the 'ideological allies' of the 'right wing of the Conservative Party'.[27]

The clerical union, APEX, and the electricians' union, the EETPU, proposed the main motion against Militant. They were supported from the floor by the former National Agent, Lord Underhill, the man who had first raised the Militant issue seven years earlier. Defending the tendency were Alan Sapper of the TV technicians union and the Tribunite MP Martin Flannery. Two Militant supporters were also allowed to speak—the long-standing candidates for the National Executive, Ray Apps and Pat Wall, who ironically was attending conference in his new capacity as properly endorsed prospective candidate for Bradford North. 'You cannot witch-hunt ideas,' Wall proclaimed.[28]

Michael Foot chose to wind up the debate himself—a sign of how important the issue was to him. The man who had so often been the victim of party discipline in the past refuted

Pat Wall's accusations:

> What is a witch-hunt? A witch-hunt is to pursue people, to persecute people—in the Labour Party context to expel people for crimes they have not committed or for crimes that are fantasies. I have been opposed to witch-hunts in this party, and I will be opposed to witch-hunts in this party until the day I die. I intend all the time to oppose such witch-hunts, but there is a sharp distinction between witch-hunts and real offences against the constitution.[29]

In three separate votes on the register and Militant, the leadership and the NEC were supported by margins of three to one.

But perhaps more important than the debate on the Monday afternoon were the results of the NEC elections the following morning. Thanks partly to the fact the railwaymen's leader, Sid Weighell, had failed to vote for the miners' candidate, Eric Clarke, as his union traditionally did, there was a bigger swing to the right than had been expected. For the first time in memory the right had a majority even without the support of Michael Foot or the soft left. Michael Foot would have no trouble now in getting together a majority for whatever action he wished to take. The left feared that the right would go further than Foot wanted, but the right also knew that it had been lucky: it was unlikely that it would achieve such a good position again. The more perceptive among those on the right realized they had less than twelve months in which to use their strong position before the left made an almost inevitable come-back. And to be effective the action had to be taken before Mrs Thatcher called a general election.

11

The Sacrificial Lambs

Over the years the man who had emerged as leader of the right-wingers on the NEC was John Golding. By the autumn of 1982 Golding was becoming known publicly as the hatchet man of the right. *Tribune* described him as the 'most powerful man in the Labour Party'.[1]

Golding is a fascinating character: an untidy little man who wears grey suits and has a mischievous schoolboy grin. In the Callaghan Government Golding served as a junior Minister at the Department of Employment and then stayed on the front bench for a while when Labour went into Opposition. But from 1980 until 1983 he preferred to concentrate on Labour Party matters and work in the Post Office Engineering Union, of which he is an Assistant Secretary and where he works most mornings. Very much a union man, Golding detests the middle-class activists of the new left and has a particular dislike for Tony Benn who, he confesses, was once his hero. Although he went to Keele University (reading Marx as a special subject) and even started a Ph.D. at the London School of Economics (on Thomas Hobbes), Golding hates students and intellectuals. He accepts that he himself was once an intellectual, but those days are over: 'There was a time when I read one or two books a day. Now it's one or two a year.'[2] Today Golding regards political theory as 'in the same league as crossword puzzles' and regards it as no guide to political action. He also dislikes the lifestyle of middle-class people: 'I don't mix with them. I've always found it difficult to get on with people like Peter Shore, Roy Hattersley and Shirley Williams.'[3] Golding admits that he and Militant have much in common. Both are strong defenders of the working class and see politics almost as a class war. Both appreciate the value of hard work and good political organization.

Golding's opening move after the 1982 Conference came at the first meeting of the NEC, the last Wednesday in October. When Jim Mortimer read out his proposals as to who should serve on each of the NEC sub-committees, Golding systematically deleted left-wingers and replaced them with his colleagues. The right's new majority ensured that each time Golding got his way, sometimes by voting margins of sixteen to eleven or, at the closest, fourteen to thirteen. Michael Foot took no part in the voting; he just watched as Golding clinically carried out his task. 'Michael hasn't got any guts left,' Dennis Skinner shouted across the room.[4] It was one of the most acrimonious NEC meetings in memory.

As a result Tony Benn lost his position as chairman of the Home Policy Committee and was replaced by Golding himself. On the Organization Committee right-winger Russell Tuck of the NUR replaced Eric Heffer in the chair.

The massacre of the left had been planned at a full-scale caucus meeting held by the right-wing members of the NEC. Fourteen of them agreed to meet one evening in a room at a pub near the House of Commons. Because of some error the room was double-booked, and so the group went instead to Locket's, the restaurant in nearby Marsham Street. Much to their embarrassment, whom should they see sitting, by co-incidence, in the hallway of the restaurant but Michael Foot, carefully counting heads as they filed past? Over dinner that evening the fourteen agreed on who should serve on each committee, although the lists had been drawn up in advance by some of the Shadow Cabinet advisers. The left on the NEC have met together regularly for years; for the right it was a relatively new habit. But the Locket's dinner turned out to be the only time that year that the right was to hold a full caucus meeting.

At this point it looked only a matter of weeks before a large-scale purge of Militant would be under way. The leaders of Militant were taking careful measures to try to minimize the possible damage. Although in theory the Labour Party now had both the power and the will to take strong action, in practice Militant was still in a good position. For one thing the party could expel only those whom it was sure belonged to Militant. As has been noted, the tendency had told the Hayward–Hughes inquiry that there were five people on its Editorial Board and that it had sixty-four full-time organizers.[5] In reality the Board has about ten members, and there were by this time more than 120 full-timers. Party officials did not know this, though, and the one or two people who suspected it could not prove it.

Jim Mortimer and Michael Foot had no option but to go by the figures and names supplied by Militant itself. They acted on the assumption that the five Editorial Board members they had been told about were the only Board members. As for the full-time workers, Jim Mortimer had compiled a list of about ninety names from various sources but admitted that he could not be certain how accurate or complete it was. Several different lists of Militant staff were being passed around at this time. One, with seventy-eight names, had been sent anonymously to Jim Mortimer, apparently by a former Militant employee. *The Times* also received a copy and at one point was going to publish it but decided not to at the last minute because the paper was not sure of the list's accuracy. In fact the collection of names, though entirely accurate, was two or three years out of date, and some of those named no longer worked for Militant.

Militant had the upper hand at this period. The tactic that the tendency employed was to focus attention on the five named members of the Editorial Board and thus to deflect inquiries about the parliamentary candidates. The five were almost sacrificial lambs. It hardly mattered if they were expelled—Taaffe and Grant had not been to a local party meeting for years anyway, though the other three were more active. The tactic worked.

Already the eight parliamentary candidates had begun deliberately to distance themselves publicly from Militant. In May 1982 the shares in WIR Publications Limited that were held by Pat Wall, Terry Harrison and Tony Mulhearn were transferred to Ted Grant, Clare Doyle and Keith Dickinson. The Militant candidates denied any formal link with the tendency and claimed merely to be readers of the paper. It was all part of a careful effort by Militant to reduce the damage of any possible disciplinary action and to present a more acceptable public image. When John Spellar stood in the Birmingham Northfield by-election Militant offered him assistance, when only weeks before, in Blackpool, Spellar had seconded the motion in support of the register (earning the name 'Ex-Spellar' from Peter Taaffe). An important part of this new approach was improved relations between Militant and the media, which naturally led to more favourable coverage.

Until this point the press and television had played a crucial part in the campaign against Militant. Many of the press 'exposés' and 'revelations' had actually been fuelled by members of the Labour Party. For instance, Lord Underhill had provided the press with copies of his 1980 report and evidence, in the hope that media coverage would increase pressure on the Labour Party NEC, and Underhill was always willing to help journalists in their work on Militant. Labour MP Frank Field is another who admits to having used the media in his campaign against the tendency.

The media coverage had been useful to Militant's enemies in two ways. First, it had helped to inform Labour Party members at all levels about just how extensive and organized Militant was. Second, it had been used by the right to force moves against Militant. The more Militant's activities in the party were publicly revealed, the more this exposure had pressurized the leadership to act, if only in the interests of preserving Labour votes. But this did not so much mean taking action against Militant as being *seen* to take it. In the end the media coverage of Militant had become so extensive that Michael Foot—who had once come to Militant's defence—was forced into taking measures against it.

Until 1982 Militant's press relations had been almost non-existent; like many organizations in the labour movement, the tendency was suspicious of the media. Interviews were given, but journalists never found Militant particularly forthcoming or informative. There was never any question of an off-the-record briefing.

In mid-1982 things changed. In June Militant appointed a press officer called Pat Edlin. He had no experience of journalism beyond a few articles in *Militant*, but after reading Denis MacShane's book *Using the Media* Edlin started building up a series of contacts in Fleet Street and broadcasting. He drank with them and had lunches and dinners, all at their expense. Edlin telephoned his contacts regularly rather than wait for the press to call him. Above all Edlin got to know journalists and quickly learned who was hostile and who was not, who needed exclusive stories to help his or her career and who did not. During the Blackpool Conference Edlin spent every evening doing the rounds of the hotel bars. People could not believe at first that he was a Militant member: he had none of the characteristics normally associated with members of the tendency. If asked an embarrassing question, Edlin would evade it rather than lie. He could tell a joke and was good company.

> He was the best press officer I've ever come across [says Richard Evans of *The Times*]. He made press men in Whitehall or the big companies look like beginners. He ought to give lessons in it.[6]

After Blackpool Martin Linton wrote in the *Guardian*:

> Militant's attitude to the press was markedly different. . . . Political journalists who had spent half a lifetime knocking Militant were bemused by [Edlin's] helpfulness, and the *Express* political editor could be seen in the bar of the Imperial Hotel one night, deep in conversation with Mr Edlin and one of Militant's parliamentary candidates. . . . he was suspected of being a public relations man, fresh from a Mayfair agency.[7]

During the autumn and winter Edlin had an exhausting time. Militant had become such a big story that he could not keep up with all his contacts: he had to be selective. The *Sun*, the *Star*, the *Mail* and the *Express* came bottom of his priorities, along with BBC TV News, which was particularly difficult to interest. Top priority were *The Times* and the *Guardian*, simply because they were the papers read by Michael Foot and most NEC members. His main television outlets were BBC 2's *Newsnight* and ITN's *News at Ten*, the programmes that Labour activists were most likely to watch late each evening after coming home from being active.

Edlin's work began to infuriate Labour Party officials. 'He made them look like idiots,' says one Fleet Street journalist. 'Mortimer and co. would produce these papers marked "private and confidential"; next day they'd be on the front page of *The Times* or the *Guardian* before most of the NEC had even seen them.'[8] Before each meeting of the NEC or the Organization Committee, Militant's photocopier was working non-stop printing the leaked papers. The street outside began to resemble Silverstone as dispatch riders waited to rush the latest set of confidential documents back to Fleet Street.

Militant's new 'cosiness with the media' (as the *Scotsman* put it) meant that press coverage was less hostile and, in some cases, almost sympathetic to the tendency. And whatever the Labour Party decided to do now had to be seen to be fair. By embarrassing Jim Mortimer in the pages of the quality press and on television, Militant was restricting his room for manoeuvre.

Immediately after Blackpool Militant made another clever move: it applied to join the register in spite of the fact that the Hayward–Hughes report had said that it would be ineligible for registration. In Militant's application Peter Taaffe confirmed that in future the annual *Militant* readers' rally would be open to Labour Party members and the press. He even offered to provide a list of Militant's full-time workers, provided that it would not be used as a basis for expulsions, and to allow Militant's accounts to be inspected. Taaffe then asked what other changes the NEC wanted Militant to make.

After complaining that Militant was being treated unfairly by comparison with other groups, Peter Taaffe revealed that Militant had taken legal advice which argued that the NEC's action was 'unconstitutional and could be subject to review in the courts'.[9] It was a sign that Militant was suddenly thinking of legal action. A Labour Party member from Liverpool, who was a lawyer, had written to Taaffe to point out that there was a strong case for legal action against the party. Settling internal problems in the 'capitalist courts' has always been frowned on within the labour movement, but Militant was about to have serious action taken against it. Furthermore, looking at it from Militant's point of view, there was an interesting precedent. Three years earlier John Golding had taken legal action against *Militant* when the newspaper had mistakenly alleged that Golding had voted against the policy of the thirty-five-hour week at a NEC meeting. Tony Benn told the NEC in November that if he had been in the same position, he too would have gone to court.

The rest of the left was mortified by the Conference decision in favour of the register. Before Conference many groups had boycotted the register, but how could the Campaign for Labour Party Democracy and others on the left now oppose a Conference decision when for so long they had been arguing about the importance of Conference policy? The question had caused a major argument during the campaign. Acerbic comments appeared in the pages of Campaign for Labour Party Democracy literature, and the group degenerated into sectarianism.

The far left was also divided in its campaign against the so-called witch-hunt. At the end of October more than 300 delegates from constituencies and trade unions met in London to form a group which called itself Labour Against the Witch-Hunt. Over 100 Militant members had gone along to try to persuade the meeting not to form a group but to channel its energies into Militant's own organization, the Labour Steering Committee Against the Witch-Hunt. The rest of the left was becoming increasingly annoyed by Militant's independent attitude and was furious with the tendency's sudden application to register, which undermined its own boycott, but it felt that it had to oppose all expulsions as a matter of principle. As for Militant itself, it was managing to deal with its own problems extremely well.

When the new Organization Sub-Committee met for the first time early in November, it agreed to a plan of action against Militant proposed by Mortimer. First, the five members of the Militant Editorial Board would be expelled from the Labour Party. Then those paid 'sales organizers' (again using Militant's phraseology) who were known would be asked if they would stop working for Militant. The eight Militant parliamentary candidates would be asked to undertake to withdraw their support for the tendency; the National Youth Committee and Youth Officer (Andy Bevan) would be asked to give a similar undertaking.[10] No mention was made of what would happen if these people did not give their assurances. The assumption was that they would be expelled. By the time the Organization Sub-Committee's report reached the full Executive, however, Jim Mortimer had been forced to change his tactics completely.[11] In between the two meetings he had received legal advice which had been obtained by a Shadow Cabinet member, John Smith.

People on the right had long been worried about the possibility that Militant might take legal action. They feared that this would be time-consuming and would delay effective action against the tendency. It would also be costly and extremely embarrassing, especially if the party lost.

Several people associated with the right-wing Labour Solidarity Campaign had thought of this possibility long before the Hayward–Hughes inquiry even reported. Then, after the Blackpool Conference, John Smith got together with other Solidarity supporters and decided that independently they would seek legal advice from a sympathetic barrister, Alexander Irvine, QC. Irvine told them that, given Mortimer's proposals, Militant would have a strong case if the tendency took legal action. For Jim Mortimer the news came as a bombshell. Quickly he had to revise his proposals so that they would be watertight in any court of law.

The register was shelved as a means of expulsion, though not discarded altogether. The target for action was narrowed down to the five members of Militant's Editorial Board. The parliamentary candidates and full-time workers seemed to be out of danger, at least for the time being. This, of course, was exactly what Militant wanted, although the last thing it could do was admit this in public. At the November NEC meeting Mortimer proposed that Militant should first be deemed ineligible for affiliation to the Labour Party—the same

191

argument that had been used in the old days to justify the Proscribed List under which Mortimer himself had once been expelled from the party; only then would Militant's Editorial Board be expelled. After the NEC meeting, however, Mortimer acknowledged that because of the legal difficulties it was 'impossible to answer' whether the party would ever be able to expel anybody.

Between November 1982 and February 1983 successive meetings of the NEC and its Organization Sub-Committee had to steer a careful course through what they saw as a legal minefield.

In December 1982, on the day that the NEC was due to declare that Militant was ineligible for affiliation, the tendency applied for a High Court injunction to prevent any action from proceeding. The Editorial Board argued that it had not been given a chance to see any of the evidence against it. (In reality, of course, Militant had a pretty good idea of nearly everything in the famous trunk at Walworth Road.) Though sympathetic to its case, Mr Justice Nourse decided against the Editorial Board. He argued that Militant should have made its legal move three months earlier, before the party Conference had reached its decision.[12] Before Blackpool the tendency had never even thought of going to court; even if it had, the idea would have been dismissed simply because it would have lost the tendency support at Conference, especially if the evidence had been made public.

The five Editorial Board members turned up at Walworth Road to appear before the NEC—the Executive was by this time concerned to be seen to be according them natural justice—but their appearance was limited to brief statements by the five; for legal reasons NEC members were told not to ask questions. Dennis Skinner stomped out of the meeting, calling it both a 'kangaroo court' and an 'example of Star Chamber procedures'.[13] The Committee then agreed that the tendency was ineligible for affiliation to the party, but expulsions could be made only once the NEC had agreed on a definition of Militant membership. The final decision had been delayed again.

Deciding who was a member of the Militant organization was not easy. The leaders of Militant denied that there was even an organization. It had been much simpler in the days of the Proscribed List, as one NEC paper commented: 'Proscribed organizations did not normally deny their existence. They had formal membership.'[14]

As the tale dragged on, it looked increasingly as if the NEC would never manage to expel anybody. The final decision was constantly delayed from one meeting to the next. At one point Jim Mortimer considered the option of avoiding expulsions altogether and trying instead to persuade Militant to dissolve the organization.[15] The General Secretary was becoming more and more frustrated by the legal problems and was particularly annoyed that every move he made was being leaked to Militant and, furthermore, covered extensively in the pages of the newspapers and on TV. In time journalists began to tire of rewriting the same story and attempting to make it look new every time, and they were annoyed about the number of cold mornings they spent sitting on the steps at Walworth Road.

On 23 February 1983, five months after the Blackpool Conference, fourteen months after the Hayward–Hughes inquiry had been set up and thirty-three years after Ted Grant had rejoined the Labour Party, it finally happened. The five Editorial Board members were called in front of the NEC for a second time and expelled. Again, no questions were asked.

The following day saw the famous Bermondsey by-election—the worst by-election result for Labour during the 1979 Parliament. A Labour majority of 38.7 per cent over the Conservatives was converted into a 31.7 per cent majority for the Liberals over Labour. Michael Foot's denunciation of

Peter Tatchell fourteen months before and the long battle over his candidature, together with an atrocious campaign of personal abuse directed against Tatchell by most of Fleet Street, contributed to a defeat which put the party in serious jeopardy. Tatchell's campaign had got off to a disastrous start when Walworth Road impounded 25,000 election leaflets that the Bermondsey party had had printed on Militant's presses at a cost of £450. (The leaflets are now prized possessions: one went for £36.50 at the 1983 Conference *Tribune* rally.) Tatchell pointed out that the local party had been printing with Militant for three years simply because it was cheaper, but he should have anticipated the reaction: he had been warned not to use Militant not only by Labour's National Agent but also by people in Militant, who believed it might be picked on by the media. In the end Tatchell ended up wasting £450 of his election expenses, and the leaflet was reprinted without the minuscule Cambridge Heath Press imprint.

After the election Tatchell complained that he had lost support during the campaign through being wrongly associated with Militant. But, inconsistently, he refused to accept that Militant was electorally damaging to Labour. The left argued that the Militant expulsions the day before polling had also lost votes. Even if this were so, by the time of the NEC meeting Tatchell had effectively already lost.

Immediately after the expulsion meeting the five held a press conference to announce the start of a campaign to secure reinstatement. Posters had even been printed in advance. Later that day, when the five returned to Militant's headquarters at Mentmore Terrace, they were almost euphoric, partly because they were relieved that the fight was over for the time being but also because they had managed to protect the people that mattered, the parliamentary candidates, and because no effective measures had yet been taken against the tendency.

From their point of view, they had virtually won the battle.

There were many on the right of the party who also felt that Militant had done very well. One Shadow Cabinet political adviser said later: 'Militant had won—game, set and match.'[16] In spite of their supposedly firm majority on the NEC, the right had been almost totally ineffectual, not just because of Militant's legal action and clever tactics but also because of its own internal divisions and lack of a clear strategy. What it had lacked above all was a good dose of democratic centralism.

Since October 1982 the right had been able to count on about sixteen votes on the Executive, but among those sixteen members there had been subtle divisions, not always understood by those outside. The most important split could be characterized as a division between the trade union 'leadership loyalists' and the parliamentary hard-liners.

The trade unionists always wanted to act cautiously. As long-serving union officials, most of them understood the importance of sticking to union rule books and of not acting too hastily. Also they did not want to embarrass Michael Foot. Most of the parliamentarians, on the other hand, wanted to act straight away and to make use of their strong but probably temporary majority on the NEC before the run-up to a general election. This meant that they sought firm and swift action against Militant on organizational matters and on policy, even if that sometimes meant countering the wishes of Michael Foot, as it had over the committee memberships. The parliamentary group wanted at least to expel all Militant's full-time organizers and parliamentary candidates. None of these NEC members had been on the National Executive long; all were marginal candidates, who might lose their seats in the future. They knew that it would only take a small shift back to the left for them to lose their places. For the trade unionists there was much less urgency; they were more certain of their positions simply because they were the nominees of large unions that never failed to get their people elected.

Working behind the scenes for the parliamentary right was a group of largely unknown people with considerable influence: the advisers to Shadow Cabinet ministers, called the 'Chocolate Soldiers' (because they were originally funded with money from the Rowntree Trust). They had tried to play a key role in the battle. Prominent among them were three in particular: Richard Heller, Denis Healey's adviser; Tony Page, adviser to both Eric Varley and Gerald Kaufman; and Patrick Cheney, who works for Denis Howell. It was they who had drawn up the lists of committee members agreed by the October caucus at Locket's.

The Locket's meeting was the last time the right ever met together as a whole group, however. John Golding and some of the other trade unionists resented the work of the political advisers. When a memo produced by Richard Heller was pinned up on a noticeboard in the Commons, Golding was furious. He told the MPs that the trade unionists wanted the Shadow Cabinet advisers excluded from future discussions and said they did not like receiving instructions from outsiders. From this point onwards the right was in disarray, depending entirely on Golding to co-ordinate its work. It was Golding who had the job of holding the right together, meeting the MPs at Westminster and talking to his fellow trade unionists on the phone. The NEC right-wingers never sorted out a programme of action for their time on the NEC. Often they decided what to do at the last minute before each meeting or even at the meetings themselves.

This would not have mattered if the right had not been divided internally. Some right-wing NEC members took a hard line on everything. Golding, while he wanted strong action, appreciated that this might not be possible. His main preoccupation, as chairman of the Home Policy Committee, was to hammer out an agreed programme on which to fight the election. He would have loved to expel the Militant candidates and full-timers but realized that the legal constraints compelled the party to proceed with caution. Privately Golding hoped that Militant would take the NEC through a long court action so that the evidence could be publicly revealed. Quite a few NEC right-wingers blame John Golding for not taking more advantage of the majority they had on the NEC and feel very strongly that bad planning on Golding's part allowed Militant to get away. Some regret that they left it to Golding to co-ordinate their work, and privately one or two now feel that they might be better off without him.

Golding argues that he did all he could in the circumstances. Above all, he points out, the right's majority was by no means as strong as the press had indicated. Many among the right-wing majority liked to act independently; some had to take into account the wishes of their unions. And the group was divided over the approach that should be adopted towards Militant. For instance, there was an argument over what to do with the evidence against Militant in the famous Walworth Road trunk. Many considered it too libellous to publish; others believed that publication would strengthen their case; most had probably never seen it anyway. In the end it was never published, much to Militant's relief. Another problem was that some right-wingers were concerned that Militant should be given a fair hearing and that natural justice should be seen to be done; others took the attitude that the case against the tendency had already been proved and that action should be swift.

If the right had been determined, there is little doubt that the parliamentary candidates could have been dropped. The NEC can choose to abandon any candidate it likes and can override the wishes of the constituency party concerned. The problem then would have been the reaction of local parties, and ultimately the NEC would probably have had to impose its own candidates upon the constituencies. As far as Militant was concerned, all the right could do was to follow the cautious lead of Jim Mortimer and Michael Foot, whose main concern was to get out of a difficult situation while being seen publicly to take action.

Boundary changes meant that only five Militant candidates eventually contested the general election. Michael Foot managed to be seen during the campaign with four of them. On the day the Labour Leader went to share a platform in Bradford with Pat Wall the Conservatives published full-page newspaper advertisements in which they reprinted part of Pat Wall's famous 'bloodshed' speech.[17]

Bradford North fell to the Conservatives after Ben Ford stood as an Independent and split the Labour vote. But on the night that Labour seats were falling everywhere two Militant candidates were returned to Parliament: David Nellist in Coventry South-East and Terry Fields in Liverpool Broadgreen, where he recorded a remarkable 4.8 per cent swing to Labour (though in Broadgreen Labour may have benefited from a split in the Alliance between their official candidate, Richard Crawshaw, and an unofficial Liberal). Around Britain that night most Labour supporters were in despair. Not members of Militant, though—they were delighted with their two successes.

John Golding returned to the Commons as MP for Newcastle-under-Lyme with a reduced majority of just under 3,000. But Golding's days as boss of the Labour right were numbered. Earlier in the week of the general election, at the conference of his union, the Post Office engineers, the broad left had taken over the union's Executive after years of control by the right. Prominent among those elected was Phil Holt, convener of the union's broad left and a member of Militant. A month later the union Executive decided that in

1983 it would not be nominating John Golding for election to the NEC of the Labour Party.

Contrast the methods of the new broad left of the Post Office engineers' Executive with those of the right-wingers on the Labour NEC. It had taken Golding months to deal with Militant, but it had taken just one meeting for Militant and its allies to deal with him.

12

Conclusion

There are many reasons why the Labour Party lost the 1983 election and why it lost so badly. Among other things, people could not accept the idea of Michael Foot as Prime Minister; many of Labour's policies were not credible with the voters; and the party's electoral organization was a shambles. But during the period when the NEC could perhaps have been dealing with these and other problems, much of its time was spent arguing about Militant. People as far apart politically as Denis Healey and Ted Grant have complained that in the year leading up to June 1983 four of the Executive's monthly meetings had been devoted almost entirely to the issue, not to mention much of the discussion at other meetings of the NEC and its sub-committees.

After a defeat as disastrous as that of June 1983 one might have expected Labour's NEC to hold an immediate inquiry on what had gone wrong: but no. At its meeting in July 1983 discussion on a post mortem report by Jim Mortimer was postponed until the autumn. Instead the NEC virtually carried on from where it had left off before the election, as if nothing had happened. Again Militant was the most important item on the agenda. The Executive followed up the expulsion of the five Editorial Board members with a ban on sales of *Militant* at Labour Party meetings and decided to stop Militant from using any party facilities in future.

If Labour ever forms another Government, the 1983 Conference in Brighton will probably be seen as an important turning-point in the party's fortunes. For the first time in years the annual assembly ended in a buoyant mood. The election of Neil Kinnock to the leadership with more than two-thirds of the electoral college votes, and of Roy Hattersley as his deputy, created a remarkable feeling of unity. Delegates believed that the party's divisions were being healed at last. But even in Brighton the Militant issue would not go away.

On the Monday, the day after the leadership election, the five expelled members of Militant's Editorial Board arrived at the Brighton Conference Centre to appeal against their expulsions. The press was excluded from the special private session, in which each of the five was given five minutes to argue for reinstatement. 'You can have unity or a witch-hunt,' Taaffe warned Conference, 'but you can't have both.'[1]

As expected, though, the Conference decided to uphold the expulsions one by one. The votes were all about three to one—roughly the same margin as for the Hayward–Hughes report and the register the year before—with the unions overruling the pro-Militant majority in the constituencies. The publicity generated by the election of Neil Kinnock and the exclusion of journalists and TV cameras meant that this latest episode in the Militant story received less coverage than it might otherwise have done.

Brighton in 1983 showed how isolated the far left of the party had suddenly become. Militant was even more on its own. At the last minute the two Militant candidates, Pat Wall and Terry Fields, announced that they were withdrawing from the NEC elections. Militant said that it was for the sake of 'left unity' and to prevent the election of right-wingers, but this consideration had never been important in previous years. Cynics said that it was because the poll would have shown a big drop in the Militant vote, since the new system of recorded voting would have ensured that Militant no longer picked up support from delegates who in the past had secretly broken the mandates from their constituency parties. But a vote might also have indicated that Militant had lost some sympathy among the local parties, which can always be counted on to vote overwhelmingly with the left. In 1983 more than 90 per cent of them voted for Tony Benn in the NEC elections; only about two-thirds supported Militant in the expulsion debate.

The party leadership's campaign against Militant had made many Labour activists more aware of the size and nature of the Militant organization. More important, the tendency lost friends by resorting to legal action, always disliked by the labour movement. In addition, Militant annoyed many party activists by the arrogant attitude that it adopted during the 1983 election campaign. The five constituencies with Militant candidates were treated by the tendency almost as if they were the only seats that mattered. Hundreds of Militant members were bussed in to these constituencies, often from marginal seats. One group of local party members said of Brighton Kemptown, where the Militant candidate Rod Fitch was standing: 'Local Labour activists were deliberately alienated from the campaign and discouraged from canvassing.... the main part of the campaign was to sell the paper and recruit to Militant.'[2] From several places reports came in of agents and candidates who had had to tell Militant members to stop selling their paper on the doorsteps while canvassing. In Edinburgh Leith the Labour agent told Militant members to go away, even though his candidate, the far-left MP Ron Brown, had once been a Militant member and is still very sympathetic to the organization. In David Nellist's seat, Coventry South-East, Militant so annoyed party members that a vote of censure was passed against the agent for the way in which ordinary party members were treated by the tendency during the campaign. When David Nellist was chosen as candidate the seat was a Militant stronghold, but the MP may have difficulty when it comes to reselection.

A sign perhaps of how much of the sympathy of the left Militant had lost came when the far left's candidate for the deputy leadership, Michael Meacher, felt able to say he would not be too concerned if the five members of the Editorial Board were not reinstated. But Militant will undoubtedly survive this temporary setback and has recently recognized the need to change its tactics, appreciating the greater hostility among Labour activists. Accepting privately that it will be difficult to make much further progress within the Labour Party in the immediate future, the tendency has stepped up its work in the trade unions, and more and more space in *Militant* is devoted to industrial matters. After the broad left's triumph at the Post Office Engineering Union conference in 1983, Militant members played a leading role in the union's campaign against the privatization of British Telecom. At the moment Militant is still relatively weak in the union movement: its public meeting at the 1983 Trades Union Congress Conference attracted only eighty people, compared with hundreds at the Labour Conference meeting. The only union it controls fully is the small Bakers' Union, but through work in the broad left groups that have been springing up in many unions over the past few years Militant could make even more progress than it has made in the Labour Party. The Post Office Engineering Union and the civil service union, the CPSA, illustrate how effective work in such broad left groups can be (although Militant lost the presidency of the CPSA in 1983). Militant's small successes have often occurred when a union has been involved in industrial action and has been unsuccessful. Mrs Thatcher's second period of office could well provide Militant with plenty of such opportunities.

The tendency has also become more active in non-party

groups. In Blackburn, for instance, where Militant has been working to replace the Labour MP Jack Straw with a Militant candidate, the tendency has become involved in local Asian organizations and has even taken over a campaign for a local well-woman centre. Such work is aimed at finding a new seam of potential recruits among the politically uncommitted. Once won over, these people will be persuaded to join the party and to support Militant in its political battles.

Another important area of work in future will be Further Education colleges, where Militant hopes to build sufficient student support to enable it eventually to win back the Labour student organization, NOLS. The tendency has also initiated campaigns founded on increasing discontent with the government's new Youth Training Scheme (YTS). YTS is condemned as the exploitation of young people and as 'cheap labour'. In particular Militant has drawn attention to the bad health and safety record of both YTS and its predecessor, the Youth Opportunities Programme. The tendency's two MPs, David Nellist and Terry Fields, have been among the YTS's biggest critics in Parliament, and the LPYS's Youth Trade Union Rights' Campaign is being used as another means of drawing into Militant young people who might not otherwise be attracted by Labour politics.

Neil Kinnock and Jim Mortimer were making it known at the Brighton Conference in 1983 that the expulsion of the five members of the Editorial Board would be the end of the measures against Militant. But moves against the tendency have since been made at local level. In Blackburn six Militant members were expelled as a result of a report submitted to the local party by a former Militant member and local councillor, Michael Gregory. (In the autumn of 1982 Gregory had 'leaked' information about Militant to certain members of the NEC but was eventually forced to leave the tendency.) Though not entirely accurate, his report provided a fascinating picture of life in Militant and exposed the organization's activities in the town, in particular its campaign to get rid of Jack Straw. At the same time the party in Gillingham suspended a local Militant member for selling *Militant* at party meetings.

Blackburn and Gillingham are isolated examples, though, and most local parties seem to have ignored the NEC's ban on the sale of *Militant*. In most constituency Labour parties the tendency will be able to continue its activities in much the same way as before.

It should be noted that Neil Kinnock seems to dislike Militant even more strongly than Michael Foot did, and during the leadership campaign he was not afraid to condemn the tendency. More than once he spoke of Militant's 'democratic centralism in antagonism to democratic socialism' and stressed that the party's 'parameters' must be safeguarded:

'If not, we're not a political party, we're a darts club.'[3] Many of Kinnock's close advisers have been among Militant's fiercest critics in the past: several were involved in student politics and Clause 4 during the mid-1970s. In spite of what he said after his election, Neil Kinnock will eventually be forced to return to the question of Militant.

The new Labour leader is known to be worried about Militant's stranglehold on the LPYS. When previous factions, such as the *Advance!* group in the 1930s, or *Keep Left* in the early 1960s, ran the party's youth section there were at least strong groups in opposition to them, but in the LPYS now opposition is tiny. Meetings are virtually indistinguishable from public meetings of Militant, and the LPYS conference amounts to a Militant rally. The LPYS should ideally provide the Labour Party with the activists, councillors, MPs and officials of the future; today LPYS leaders are almost guaranteed to go on to distinguished careers in Militant, not the Labour Party.

Kinnock will also come under pressure when Labour constituencies go through the next round of reselections of sitting MPs, due to start at the end of 1984. Militant is hoping to exploit the process much more than it did last time and will again be concentrating its efforts on certain constituencies. In spite of the expulsions in Blackburn, Jack Straw is still under threat, and Militant is likely to move against another fervent critic on the soft left, Frank Field, in Birkenhead. The tendency could also do well in some of the Glasgow seats, where there are elderly right-wing MPs. In some reselection battles Militant will simply contribute towards the choice of a candidate more left-wing than the sitting MP; in others it will try to get its own man chosen with a view to increasing its team in the Commons, as it has promised.

In terms of members and money Militant is in a much better position than ever before and seems to have gained hundreds of members during the witch-hunt period. The tendency's membership will probably continue to grow, though not as rapidly as in recent years: for reasons of diplomacy Militant will lie low for a while after the intense period of the Foot leadership. It must consolidate its position in the Labour Party, concentrating on new areas of work, raising the money and preparing the ground for the daily paper that it hopes to launch shortly.

Many people, especially those on the left, argue that Militant's significance has been greatly exaggerated by right-wingers and journalists. Peter Hain wrote in 1983:

Its supporters on the one hand and the party's right and the media on the other each had a vested interest in exaggerating the group's influence. Militant has thrived on being pilloried and on the false impression that it virtually is the Labour left. In fact it is simply one of the groups operating within the party, and has hardly contributed at all to the democratic and policy changes adopted over the past ten years. . . .[4]

Militant's membership of about 4,700 may look insignificant compared with the 274,000 individual Labour Party members. But, as we have seen, a relatively small group of very active people can exert considerable influence. Militant's members, all of them highly active, should really be compared with the estimated 55,000 or so Labour Party activists (probably an exaggeration),[5] but even that comparison is not really valid, since a Militant member will generally be far better organized and more active than the average Labour Party worker. Through good organization and hard work Militant has made its small membership pay large dividends. This can be seen every year at Labour Party Conferences. As early as 1976 Militant boasted internally that one-third of the constituency speeches at Conference came from Militant members, though the tendency had only forty constituency delegates out of nearly 600.[6] The trend has continued in recent years—in 1983 one prominent Militant member, Tony Mulhearn, managed to speak four times. This disproportionate influence is the product of careful planning in the constituencies so that Militant people are selected as conference delegates, of good lobbying during the pre-Conference composite meetings to make sure that Militant members propose or second the composited motions, and of the caucus meetings that are held every evening during Conference to decide which Militant delegates will volunteer to speak in which debates. Militant will never be in a position to take over the Labour Party completely, and in any case that is not its aim. The party is regarded simply as fertile territory in which to recruit the vanguard for the revolution. And as long as it continues to do this Militant will be a severe irritation for the Labour leadership.

Militant's stewardship of the party's 'front door', the LPYS, has dissuaded thousands of young recruits from joining the party. Its insistence on total commitment from its members, who are always discouraged from taking on onerous positions in the party, has deflected vital energy and enthusiasm. The tendency often burns out idealistic young people who join the party and get sucked into Militant straightaway. Many of them become disillusioned with politics long before they have a chance to become involved in the Labour Party itself. Militant's income of more than £1 million a year has undoubtedly diverted funds that might otherwise have been given to the party itself and which Walworth Road badly needs.

During the early years of its existence Militant faced no competition from other Trotskyist groups in the party: there were none. But its success in the last few years has encouraged other Trotskyists to move in, though at the moment, apart from those in London, none has anything like Militant's strength. The main Trotskyist rivals to Militant are the *Socialist Organizer* group and the Socialist League, neither of which has more than 1,000 members or any strength outside London. Politically both are more in tune with the far left of the Labour Party than with Militant and are much more interested in the kind of 'middle-class' issues that Militant shuns, such as feminism, race, gay rights and Ireland. Like Militant, both groups are Marxist–Leninist bodies with secret organizations. By comparison with Militant, these Trotskyist groups inside the party, and several other even smaller ones, are still relatively insignificant and influential in only a handful of constituencies. None is anything like as well organized as Militant or as entrenched in the party. It is unlikely that they will reach Militant's size or strength. Militant, with nearly 5,000 members, considerable financial resources and control of the LPYS, has a long head-start.

Until recently the campaign against Militant centred on the argument that it was a 'party within a party', with a separate organization and policies. While this is undoubtedly true of Militant, the argument is a weak one. There are dozens of groups within the Labour Party that have the characteristics of political parties—Labour Solidarity and the Labour Co-ordinating Committee, for instance. But what has only recently been understood is that the important distinction between these pressure groups and Militant is the nature of Militant's organization. Neil Kinnock is right when he says that it is Militant's democratic centralism that constitutes the essential difference. Neither Labour Solidarity nor the Labour Co-ordinating Committee is a democratic centralist group; nor were the Bevanites in the 1950s. These groups do not decide on their policies in secret and then unite to present an agreed line to the outside world. Indeed, they suffer from the exposure of too many of their internal disagreements in public.

Members of Militant are never seen to dissent from the tendency line. Public consistency is so complete that Militant members can always be identified immediately because they use the same arguments, language, metaphors and even hand movements in putting forward the tendency's views. Discipline is very strict. Militant has not the slightest hesitation in expelling people from its ranks, not just for disagreeing publicly over policy but also for offences such as smoking pot or failing to attend meetings regularly. It is ironic that the tendency should complain of a Labour Party witch-hunt when Militant itself quite frequently resorts to expulsions. Coincidentally, Militant even allows its expelled dissenters to appeal to its own national conference, in exactly the same way as the Militant five were allowed to appeal to the Labour Party Conference at Brighton. Militant's Leninist style of organization, with iron discipline and complete secrecy, is wholly alien to the democratic and open traditions of the Labour Party. Those Labour Party members who defend Militant fail to recognize that few of them would last five minutes in the unlikely event of the Labour Party's being taken over by Militant.

It is one thing to decide that Militant has no place in the Labour Party, however, and quite another matter to do something about it, as recent events have shown. If Militant could ever have been killed off, it was when it was small. That opportunity was lost in 1975, when Reg Underhill's first report on the tendency was virtually ignored. In retrospect one can see that Militant's progress would have been blocked if the Labour Party had closed down the LPYS at that point. Then the organization only had about 1,000 members, less than a quarter of its strength today. Its membership was concentrated largely in the Labour Party youth section, and Militant was then only just starting to make advances within the party itself. Without the LPYS Militant would have been shattered. But in 1975 such action would never have been sanctioned by the left-wing majority on the NEC. Not even Underhill believed that such a drastic move was necessary. By the time the NEC had the will to act against Militant, the tendency was a far stronger and more difficult opponent. By the late 1970s it had gained strength in a large number of constituency parties and sympathetic support from the far left, which was now stronger and better organized. If the LPYS were closed down now, Militant would survive, and even today's more right-wing National Executive would be unlikely to agree to such a move.

The legal and procedural battles of 1982 and 1983 showed that the NEC is virtually powerless to take action against a group which has burrowed secretly right into the party. Given the present Labour Party rules, it would be possible for the National Front to disband, enter the Labour Party and operate secretly inside. Indeed, there is some evidence that this is exactly what some groups of former National Front members have done within the Conservative Party,[7] and the Conservatives seem to have been equally unable to deal with their own entrist problem.

The decentralized nature of the Labour Party has been another major stumbling-block in the way of action against Militant. Local constituency parties have a remarkable amount of autonomy. Ultimately it is the constituencies that decide whether or not to accept applications for Labour Party membership and that determine who will be parliamentary candidates. The NEC may make decisions on these matters but is virtually powerless if a constituency party decides otherwise, unless the NEC takes the drastic step of closing down that particular local party. The Peter Tatchell and Pat Wall cases illustrated this problem perfectly, and in the end the Bermondsey and Bradford North parties were able to defeat both the NEC and a party leader who later publicly supported candidates whom he had previously denounced. And even after the decisions by the NEC and the party Conference to expel the Militant five, three of them, Ted Grant, Peter Taaffe and Keith Dickinson, were still regarded as members by their local parties. No matter what the party leadership or the NEC decides in Walworth Road, nothing can be done about Militant without the co-operation of the local parties. And naturally the constituencies where Militant is strongest are the least likely to want to take any such action.

Militant's growth has been less a cause of the Labour Party's decline, as some people argue, than a result and a symptom of it. Party membership today is at a lower level than at any time since the 1930s. Militant has done well in areas where the Labour Party organization is weak, such as Liverpool, and although Militant takeovers of local parties may often prompt an increase in local Labour Party membership and activity, Militant will generally keep its grip on those parties.

In the event of a Labour Party revival, the tendency's relative importance and strength would be diminished to some extent. If people do flock back into the party and the Labour Party acquires a more active mass membership, sheer numbers will weaken Militant. Attracting more people into the party is one of the most important tasks facing Neil Kinnock. But it will not be easy. The Labour Party suffers from an activist elite which is not particularly concerned about the number of party members. In any case, while a resurgence of party membership and participation could cause Militant some discomfort, it would not kill the tendency altogether.

It is nearly ten years since the existence of this entrist group inside the Labour Party was brought to the attention of the party authorities and the public. For most of that decade no action was taken by the party because too few wanted to take it. When, more recently, enough people in positions of power changed their minds, it was too late. Militant had burrowed too deep to be extracted, and the party was ill-equipped to get rid of it.

Militant is bound to trouble the party leadership further, especially as Labour makes new efforts to regain its former strength. More Militant members will be selected as candidates in safe Labour seats and in turn will be sent to the House of Commons. Militant will gain further positions of influence and power. The press, radio and television will ensure that Militant continues to be a public embarrassment. There is little that the Labour Party can do about it now: Militant is here to stay.

Appendix 1

MILITANT CANDIDATES STANDING FOR THE LABOUR PARTY NATIONAL EXECUTIVE, 1971–1983

Militant candidates have never been successful in contests for the seven places in the constituency section of the NEC, nor have they even come close. But this section is always dominated by prominent MPs, and Militant candidates have frequently received more votes than any other candidate who is not an MP or a former MP. Over the years such well-known MPs as Joe Ashton, Bob Cryer, David Ennals, Stuart Holland, Les Huckfield, Gerald Kaufman, Stan Orme, Merlyn Rees, John Smith and Peter Shore have sometimes polled fewer votes than Militant candidates. In this period the lowest number of votes needed to secure election has ranged from 225,000 to 290,000. Apart from a handful of parties with a very high membership, each constituency has 1,000 votes.

Year	Candidate	Votes polled
1971	Ray Apps	31,000
1972	Pat Craven	51,000
1973	David Skinner	144,000[1,2]
	Ray Apps	81,000
1974	Ray Apps	54,000[1]

213

Year	Candidate	Votes polled
1975	Maureen Golby	75,000[1]
1976	David White	57,000[1]
	John Ferguson	56,000[1]
1977	Pat Wall	67,000[1]
	Ray Apps	66,000[1]
1978	Nick Bradley	97,000[1,3]
	Ray Apps	57,000[1]
	Pat Wall	51,000[1]
1979	Ray Apps	73,000
	Pat Wall	69,000
1980	Pat Wall	45,000
	Ray Apps	43,000
1981	Ray Apps	46,000
	Pat Wall	45,000
1982	Pat Wall	103,000[1,4]
1983[5]	Terry Fields MP[5]	
	Pat Wall[5]	

Notes:
[1] The highest vote(s) for any candidate(s) not an MP or a former MP.
[2] Skinner's vote was probably high because he was one of the Clay Cross councillors.
[3] Retiring LPYS NEC member.
[4] Terry Fields polled 1,305,000 votes in the trade union section.
[5] Recorded votes for the first time—withdrew in the cause of 'left unity'.

Source: Labour Party Annual Conference Reports, 1971–83.

Appendix 2

MILITANT CANDIDATES IN ELECTIONS

The following abbreviations are used below: Con—Conservative; Ecol—Ecology Party; Ind—Independent; IWRP—Isle of Wight Residents Party; Lab—Labour; Lib—Liberal; Lib/All—Liberal candidate fielded by the SDP/Liberal Alliance; NF—National Front; SDP—Social Democratic Party; SDP/All—SDP candidate fielded by the SDP/Liberal Alliance.

MAY 1979 GENERAL ELECTION
National Lab–Con swing: 5.2 per cent

CROSBY

Candidate	Votes polled	% of total
Page (Con)	34,768	56.9
Mulhearn, Tony	15,496	25.4
Hill (Lib)	9,302	15.2
Hussey (Ecol)	1,489	2.4

Swing to Con: 5.2 per cent.

CROYDON CENTRAL

Candidate	Votes polled	% of total
Moore (Con)	26,457	52.5
White, David	18,499	36.7
Johnson (Lib)	5,112	10.1
Others	354	0.7

Swing to Con: 7.7 per cent. A larger than average swing in a seat once held by Labour.

ISLE OF WIGHT

Candidate	Votes polled	% of total
Ross (Lib)	35,889	48.2
Fishburn (Con)	35,537	47.7
Wilson, Cathy	3,014	4.0

Labour's vote fell from 13 to 4 per cent, partly as a result of long-term erosion by the Liberals.

JUNE 1979 ELECTIONS TO THE EUROPEAN PARLIAMENT

LIVERPOOL

Candidate	Votes polled	% of total
Hooper (Con)	49,646	45.2
Harrison, Terry	42,419	38.7
Clark (Lib)	17,650	16.1

The swing to the Conservatives of 11 per cent, based on the general election figures of only a month before, was the largest in the country. It was partly a result of the lowest turnout in the UK, 23.7 per cent.

JUNE 1983 GENERAL ELECTION
National Lab–Con swing: 3.9 per cent

BRADFORD NORTH

Candidate	Votes polled	% of total
Lawler (Con)	16,094	34.3
Wall, Pat	14,492	30.9
Birkby (SDP/All)	11,962	25.5
Ford (Lab Ind)	4,018	8.6
Others	387	0.8

Pat Wall would have won this normally safe Labour seat had not the deselected MP, Ben Ford, stood as an Independent.

BRIGHTON KEMPTOWN

Candidate	Votes polled	% of total
Bowden (Con)	22,265	51.1
Fitch, Rod	12,887	29.6
Burke (SDP/All)	8,098	18.6
Budden (NF)	290	0.7

Swing to Con: 2.2 per cent. From 1964 to 1970 this was a Labour seat.

COVENTRY SOUTH-EAST

Candidate	Votes polled	% of total
Nellist, David	15,307	41.1
Arnold (Con)	12,625	33.9
Kilby (Lib/All)	9,323	25.0

Swing to Con: 4.2 per cent. David Nellist took over the seat from retiring Labour MP, William Wilson.

ISLE OF WIGHT

Candidate	Votes polled	% of total
Ross (Lib/All)	38,407	51.0
Bottomley (Con)	34,904	46.3
Wilson, Cathy	1,828	2.4
McDermott (IWRP)	208	0.3

Thought to be Labour's worst ever vote in a parliamentary election. Back in 1964 Labour polled 31.6 per cent of the votes, more than twice the Liberal vote.

LIVERPOOL BROADGREEN

Candidate	Votes polled	% of total
Fields, Terry	18,802	40.9
Dougherty (Con)	15,002	32.6
Pine (Ind Lib)	7,021	15.3
Crawshaw (SDP/All)	5,169	11.2

Swing to Lab: 4.8 per cent. The swing to Labour was probably aided by a split between the official SDP/Alliance candidate and an unofficial Liberal. Liverpool had an overall 2.4 per cent swing to Labour.

Appendix 3

MILITANT'S CENTRAL COMMITTEE

All members of the Central Committee have to be Militant full-timers. Apart from the ten people I suggest are on the Militant Executive (indicated below by an asterisk), my research has indicated that the following regional full-timers and bureaux organizers are so prominent within Militant that it would be surprising if they were not on the Central Committee too:

Ray Apps (Southern); Brian Beckingham (South West); Jeremy Birch (West Midlands); Nick Brooks (Southern); Laurence Coates (Youth); Dave Cotterill (North East); Pat Craven (Scotland); Margaret Creear; Keith Dickinson*; Clare Doyle* (Treasurer); Robert Edwards (Eastern Region); Robert Faulkes (London); Phil Frampton (Manchester and Lancs); Ted Grant*; Peter Hadden (Ireland); Terry Harrison (Merseyside); Brian Ingham* (Industrial); John Ingham (Yorkshire); Peter Jarvis (Industrial); Bob Labi (International); Gerry Lerner (Manchester and Lancs); John Pickard* (*Militant*); Tony Saunois* (Youth); Bob Sewell (Head Office); Roger Silverman* (International); Peter Taaffe* (General Secretary); Alex Thraves (Wales); Richard Venton (Merseyside); Lynn Walsh*; Alan Woods* (*Militant International Review*); Bob Wylie (Scotland).

Notes and References

Where the source is an internal Militant document I have indicated this by the words 'Militant int. doc.'. The tendency's internal documents have not been published anywhere in full, although P. Shipley (*The Militant Tendency*, Foreign Affairs Publishing Co., London, 1983), has published lengthy extracts from some of them. LPACR refers to the Labour Party Annual Conference Report, the account of Conference proceedings published each year a few months afterwards. NEC Report refers to the annual report submitted to the Conference by the Labour Party National Executive Committee.

The Harvester Press has an almost complete run of *Militant*, together with some of the pre-Militant 'Grantite' publications, in its microfilm collection, 'The Left in Britain' (Harvester/Primary Social Sources, Brighton) available in many academic libraries. But since this material was supplied by Militant itself, it lacks many of the earlier publications from the RCP and RSL. Some of the 'Grantite' publications from the 1930s, 1940s and 1950s can be found in the Haston Collection at the University of Hull, in the Deane Collection at Manchester Polytechnic, and in a library of Trotskyist literature at the University of Warwick.

1 'I CALL THIS AN OUTRAGE'

1 NEC Papers, April 1954.
2 *Tribune*, 13 August 1954.
3 *Tribune*, 18 June 1982, 25 June 1982 and 1 October 1982.
4 *Lenin on Britain*, Martin Lawrence, London, 1934, p. 257.
5 D. Hyde, *I Believed*, William Heinemann, London, 1950, pp. 65–6.

6 Ibid.

7 Quoted in B. Reed and G. Williams, *Denis Healey and the Policies of Power*, Sidgwick and Jackson, London, 1971, p. 25.

8 *Socialist Outlook* was never on the Proscribed List, though.

9 *Tribune*, 13 August 1954.

10 S. Hoggart and D. Leigh, *Michael Foot: a Portrait*, Hodder and Stoughton, London, 1981, p. 112.

11 LPACR, 1952, p. 87, though reported as 'your gob'.

12 Speech reported in *The Times*, 13 October 1952.

13 See I. Mikardo, *New Socialist*, March/April 1982.

14 L. Hunter, *The Road to Brighton Pier*, Arthur Barker, London, 1959, p. 8.

15 Ibid, p. 7.

16 Author's calculation based on P. Norton, *Dissension in the House of Commons*, Macmillan, London, 1975.

2 THE PERMANENT REVOLUTIONARY

1 I. Deutscher, *The Prophet Outcast*, Oxford University Press, Oxford, 1979, pp 43–4.

2 L. Trotsky, 'The Lever of a Small Group' (1933), *Writings of Leon Trotsky 1933–34*, Pathfinder, New York, 1975, pp. 125–6.

3 L. Trotsky, 'Interview with Collins' (1936), *Writings of Leon Trotsky, 1935–36*, Pathfinder, New York, 1977, pp. 379, 382.

4 T. Ali, *The Coming British Revolution*, Jonathan Cape, London, 1972, p. 139.

5 Martin Upham in his Ph.D. thesis, 'The History of British Trotskyism to 1949', University of Hull, 1980, says that Grant may have arrived as early as 1934. A revised version of the thesis is due to be published by Spokesman.

6 M. Haston (formerly Lee), interview with author.

7 *Preparing for Power*, Workers' International League, London, 1942, p. 9.

8 War Cabinet papers, 'The Trotskyist Movement in Great Britain', 13 April 1944, available at Public Records Office.

9 Ibid.

10 Ibid.

11 F. Ward, interview with author.

12 S. Bornstein, unpublished interview with Tom Forester.

13 T. Grant, rough draft of 'Letter to the Members', sent to J. Deane, February 1949, Deane Collection, Manchester Polytechnic.

14 F. Ward, interview with author.
15 Ibid.
16 J. Deane, interview with author.
17 *International Socialist*, February 1952.
18 For instance, *Militant*, 16 September 1983.
19 *Workers' International Review*, April–May 1957.
20 *Observer*, 31 August 1975.
21 'Problems of Entrism' (RSL int. doc.), March 1959.
22 'Entrism' (Militant int. doc.), November 1973.
23 *Militant*, January 1970.
24 *Socialist Fight*, January 1958.
25 *Socialist Fight*, June 1963.

3 ENTER MILITANT

1 As reported by J. Deane, interview with author.
2 *Militant*, October 1964.
3 Ibid.
4 Ibid.
5 Ibid.
6 Ibid.
7 *The Week*, no. 3, January 1964.
8 Quoted by N. Beloff in the *Observer*, 31 August 1975.
9 Letter to G. Kennedy, 6 October 1964, quoted in Beloff, op. cit.
10 Letter to G. Kennedy, December 1964, quoted in Beloff, op. cit.
11 Letter to G. Kennedy, January 1965, quoted in Beloff, op. cit.
12 Bob Pennington, quoted in Beloff, op. cit.
13 *Militant*, May 1965.
14 E. Hillman, interview with author.
15 Z. Layton-Henry, *Journal of Contemporary History*, 1976, p. 275.
16 P. Abrams and A. Little, *British Journal of Sociology*, 1965, p. 321.
17 Report of the Committee of Enquiry into Party Organization (the Simpson Committee), Labour Party, 1968, pp. 11–14.
18 N. Vann, interview with author.
19 Ibid.
20 Ibid.
21 'British Perspectives and Tasks' (Militant int. doc.), March 1972.
22 Claimed in 'CWI Bulletin', no. 1 (Militant int. doc.), July 1974.
23 LPACR, 1972, pp. 178–93.

24 LPACR, 1973, pp. 170–88.
25 LPACR, 1971, p. 156; 1972, p. 174; 1973, p. 159.
26 'British Perspectives and Tasks 1974' (Militant int. doc.), June 1974, p. 37.
27 Ibid, p. 19
28 Ibid, p. 21.

4 POLICIES AND PROGRAMME

1 A. Glyn, *Capitalist Crisis—Tribune's 'Alternative Strategy' or Socialist Plan*, Militant, London, 1983 edn, p. 71.
2 P. Taaffe, *What We Stand For*, Militant, December 1981, pp. 1–3.
3 L. Trotsky, 'The Transitional Programme' (1938), *Documents of the Fourth International*, Pathfinder, New York, 1973, p. 183.
4 Glyn, op. cit., p. 70.
5 *Militant International Review*, January 1973.
6 Taaffe, op. cit., p. 10.
7 *Sunday Times*, 7 March 1982.
8 'British Perspectives and Tasks 1974' (Militant int. doc.), June 1974, p. 33.
9 A. Woods and T. Grant, *Lenin and Trotsky—What They Really Stood For*, Militant, 1976 edn, pp. 147–8.
10 Glyn, op. cit., p. 68.
11 'Programme of the International' (Militant int. doc.), 3rd edn, January 1980, p. 16.
12 *Militant International Review*, no. 15, 1978.
13 *Militant*, 21 May 1982.
14 *Militant*, 7 May 1982.
15 *Militant*, 25 September 1981.
16 'British Perspectives 1977' (Militant int. doc.), 1977, p. 29.

5 OPERATION ICEPICK

1 NEC Papers, January 1977.
2 B. Clarke, interview with author.
3 See *Militant*, 8 April 1983.
4 See D. Kogan and M. Kogan, *The Battle for the Labour Party*, Kogan Page, London, 1983.
5 LPACR, 1939, p. 322.
6 Lord Underhill, interview with author.
7 Ibid.
8 NEC Papers, November 1975.
9 Ibid.

10 Ibid.

11 For instance, B. Castle, *The Castle Diaries*, Weidenfeld & Nicolson, London, 1980, p. 565.

12 Ibid.

13 *The Times*, 12 December 1975.

14 *Observer*, 31 August 1975.

15 *Observer*, 21 September 1975.

16 *The Times*, 21 July 1975.

17 *Political Quarterly*, 1970, p. 147.

18 *Observer*, 1 June 1975.

19 *New Statesman*, 15 October 1976.

20 See P. McCormick, *Enemies of Democracy*, Temple Smith, London, 1979.

21 Bradley lost 37–20 to a former Tribunite MP, James Dickens, who then resigned as candidate just before the 1979 election, when the Newham party refused to give overwhelming support to his election manifesto.

22 'British Perspectives and Tasks 1975' (Militant int. doc.), 1975, p. 14.

23 *Daily Telegraph*, 15 January 1977.

24 The title seems to have been used first by the *Daily Express*, 24 November 1976.

25 *Daily Telegraph*, 24 November 1976.

26 NEC Papers, January 1977.

27 *The Times*, 26 November 1976.

28 *Guardian*, 13 December 1976.

29 Ibid.

30 *The Times*, 1, 2, 3, 4, 6 December 1976.

31 Report of the Special Committee to Examine the Documents on Entrism, LPACR, 1975, pp. 383–5.

32 Reported in interviews with author by former members of Youth Committee.

6 THE ORGANIZATION

1 *Liverpool Daily Post*, 11 December 1981.

2 As reported by NEC members in interviews with author.

3 'Entrism' (Militant int. doc.), November 1973.

4 'CWI Bulletin', no. 1 (Militant int. doc.), July 1974.

5 *Militant*, 26 April 1974.

6 *Militant*, 13 June 1981.

7 Party Constitution and Standing Orders, Labour Party.

7 MILITANT'S MONEY

1 J. Kay and M. King, *The British Tax System*, OUP, Oxford, 1978, p. 199.

2 Accounts of WIR Publications Limited, 1976–7, available at Companies House.

3 T. Harrison, interview with author.

4 See letter from P. Taaffe to Labour Party General Secretary, published in NEC Report, 1982, pp. 136–9, together with *Militant*, 14 January 1983, and 13 January 1984.

5 For instance, *Militant*, 13 December 1974.

6 *Militant*, 25 October 1974.

7 *Militant*, 1 November 1974.

8 A. Woods and T. Grant, *Lenin and Trotsky—What They Really Stood For*, International Publishers, Colombo, 1972, pp. 153–72.

9 WIR Publications Limited, Articles of Association.

10 Cambridge Heath Press Limited, Articles of Association.

11 WIR Publications Limited, Register of Shareholders.

12 Accounts of WIR Publications Limited and Cambridge Heath Press Limited, although the accounts do not state specifically that the loans are from one company to the other, and there are other small loans by WIR Publications Limited.

13 WIR Publications Limited, annual accounts.

14 P. Taaffe's reply to Labour Party questionnaire, April 1980, printed in full in B. Baker, *The Far Left*, Weidenfeld & Nicolson, London, 1981, pp. 36–9.

15 WIR Publications Limited, annual accounts 1973–81.

16 Taaffe, op. cit.

17 For instance, *Militant*, 5 January, 23 February 1973.

18 Interview with author.

19 Interview with author.

20 Interview with author.

21 Noted in Hayward–Hughes report, NEC Report, 1982, pp. 133–5.

22 Claimed by ex-member Michael Gregory in his report to the Blackburn Labour Party, January 1983. Not published but reported in *The Times*, 21 February 1983, and the *Guardian*, 12 March 1983.

23 Ibid.

24 P. Tatchell, *The Battle for Bermondsey*, Heretic Books, London, 1983, p. 120.

25 Accounts of London Region of NOLS, 1977–8.
26 Gregory, op. cit.
27 Report of Houghton Committee on aid to political parties, HMSO, Cmnd 6601, 1976.
28 Estimate based on annual accounts in NEC Report and Houghton Committee estimate of constituency party incomes.
29 Interview with former Liberal Party Secretary-General.
30 Interview with SDP National Organizer.
31 Accounts of Fabian Society, Fabian Society Annual Report, 1982–3.
32 Accounts of Tribune Publications Limited, 1980–1.
33 Accounts of Campaign for Labour Party Democracy, 1982–3.

8 THE MILITANT LIFE

1 As reported by ex-members who attended.
2 As reported by ex-member.
3 D. Mason, interview with author.
4 Ibid.
5 Ibid.
6 Ibid.
7 T. McDonald, interview with author.
8 Ibid.
9 Ibid.
10 Ibid.
11 Ibid.
12 Ibid.
13 R. Hart, interview with author.
14 Ibid.
15 M. Barnes, letter to *New Statesman*, 1 February 1980.
16 Barnes, interview with author.
17 Ibid.
18 Barnes, letter.
19 Barnes, interview.
20 Barnes, letter.
21 Barnes, interview.
22 Ibid.

9 MILITANT MERSEYSIDE

1 *OPCS Monitor*, Office of Population Censuses and Surveys, October 1982.

2 M. Foot, *Sunday Mirror*, 23 November 1980.
3 T. Lane, *Marxism Today*, November 1978.
4 *New Statesman*, 31 July 1964.
5 See P. Wall, *Guardian*, 16 August 1982.
6 Simon Frazer, former Secretary of the Liverpool Labour party and Trades Council, quoted in P. J. Waller, *Democracy and Sectarianism: A Political and Social History of Liverpool 1868–1939*, Liverpool University Press, Liverpool, 1981, p. 348.
7 Robert Baxter, 'The Liverpool Labour Party, 1918–1963', unpublished D. Phil. thesis, Oxford, 1969.
8 Reported by T. Harrison, interview with author.
9 I. Craig, interview with author.
10 E. Roderick, interview with author.
11 Report of the Policy/Programme Sub-Committee of the Liverpool District Labour Party, 1982.
12 E. Roderick, interview.
13 BBC Radio *File on 4*, 30 September 1982.
14 T. Aitman, interview with author.
15 T. Lane, *Marxism Today*, February 1981.

10 FOOT STEPS FORWARD

1 T. Forester, *New Society*, 10 January 1980.
2 *Daily Mirror*, 14 January 1980.
3 *Sunday Times*, 16 December 1979.
4 *New Society*, op. cit.
5 *New Statesman*, 18 January 1980.
6 BBC 2 *Newsnight*, 31 January 1980.
7 NEC Report, 1980, p. 7.
8 Lord Underhill, interview with author.
9 Both quoted in *Sunday Times*, 20 January 1980.
10 See D. Kogan and M. Kogan, *The Battle for the Labour Party*, Kogan Page, London, 1983, for the story of the Rank and File Mobilizing Committee.
11 For instance, ITN's main news bulletin had a longer extension on the night of the deputy leadership election in 1981 than on the evening of the elections in 1983.
12 'British Perspectives and Tasks 1974' (Militant int. doc.), June 1974, p. 20.
13 *London Labour Briefing*, May 1981.
14 The *Sun*'s headline 'Furious Foot Disowns Red Pete—Militant Will Never Be an MP' (4 December 1981) is one example of

many. Long after Tatchell had made it clear that he was not a supporter of Militant, some papers referred to him as 'militant-tending' or having 'militant tendencies'. See P. Tatchell, *The Battle for Bermondsey*, Heretic Books, London, 1983, pp. 58–61.

15 Tatchell, op. cit., pp. 89, 96.
16 *Tribune*, 25 February 1983. See also article by Audrey Wise giving details of trivial items in regional staff's evidence.
17 F. Field, evidence to Labour Party inquiry.
18 *Sunday Times*, 7 March 1982.
19 Ibid.
20 Ibid.
21 *Daily Mail* and *Daily Telegraph*, 8 March 1982.
22 NEC Report, 1982, pp. 133–42.
23 *Labour Weekly*, 25 June 1982.
24 Ibid.
25 *The Times*, 28 June 1982.
26 LPACR 1982, pp. 40–53, for whole debate.
27 Ibid.
28 Ibid.
29 Ibid.

11 THE SACRIFICIAL LAMBS

1 *Tribune*, 28 January 1983.
2 J. Golding, interview with author.
3 Ibid.
4 *Guardian*, 28 October 1982.
5 NEC Report, 1982, p. 137.
6 R. Evans, interview with author.
7 *Guardian*, 18 October 1982.
8 Interview with author.
9 Militant's 'Application for Registration'; see *Militant*, 22 October 1982.
10 NEC Papers, November 1982.
11 NEC Papers (revised), November 1982.
12 *The Times*, 16 December 1982.
13 *Guardian*, 16 December 1982.
14 NEC Papers, January 1983.
15 Ibid.
16 Interview with author.
17 For instance, *Daily Express*, 28 May 1983.

12 CONCLUSION

1 Secret recording of the debate on Militant.
2 Letter to *Labour Leader*, August 1983.
3 Fabian Society Labour leadership debate, Central Hall, Westminster, 29 July 1983.
4 P. Hain, *The Democratic Alternative*, Penguin, Harmondsworth, 1983, p. 117.
5 Estimate for 1978 in P. Whiteley, *The Labour Party in Crisis*, Methuen, London, 1983, p. 55.
6 'International Bulletin' (Militant int. doc.), February 1977.
7 A report by the Young Conservatives on right-wing infiltration into the Conservative Party was leaked just before the 1983 Conservative Conference; see *Observer*, 9 October 1983. The issue was covered in more detail by BBC1, *Panorama*, 30 January 1984.

Bibliography

Ali, Tariq, *The Coming British Revolution*, Jonathan Cape, London, 1972

Baker, Blake, *The Far Left*, Weidenfeld & Nicolson, London, 1981

Benn, Tony, *Arguments for Socialism*, ed. Chris Mullin, Jonathan Cape, London, 1979

Bornstein, Sam, and Richardson, Al, *Two Steps Back*, Socialist Platform, Ilford, 1983

Braddock, Jack and Bessie, *The Braddocks*, Macdonald, London, 1963

Bradley, Ian, *Breaking The Mould? The Birth and Prospects of the Social Democratic Party*, Martin Robertson, Oxford, 1981

Castle, Barbara, *The Castle Diaries, 1974–76*, Weidenfeld & Nicolson, London, 1980

Cook, Chris, and Taylor, Ian, *The Labour Party: an Introduction to its History, Structure and Politics*, Longman, London, 1980

Crossman, Richard, *The Backbench Diaries of Richard Crossman*, ed. Janet Morgan, Hamish Hamilton and Jonathan Cape, London, 1981

Deutscher, Isaac, *The Prophet Outcast: Trotsky 1929–1940*, Oxford University Press, Oxford, 1963

Duncan, Pete, *Paved with Good Intentions: The Politics of Militant*, Clause 4, London, 1981

Foot, Michael, *Aneurin Bevan: 1897–1945*, MacGibbon & Kee, London, 1962

Foot, Michael, *Aneurin Bevan: 1945–1960*, Davis-Poynter, London, 1973

Gaitskell, Hugh, *The Diary of Hugh Gaitskell 1945–1956*, ed. P. Williams, Jonathan Cape, London, 1983

BIBLIOGRAPHY

Glyn, Andrew, *Capitalist Crisis: Tribune's Alternative Strategy or Socialist Plan*, Militant, London, 1978

Groves, Reg, *The Balham Group*, Pluto, London, 1974

Hain, Peter, *The Democratic Alternative: a Socialist Response to Britain's Crisis*, Penguin, Harmondsworth, 1983

Harris, Kenneth, *Attlee*, Weidenfeld and Nicolson, London, 1982

Haseler, Stephen, *The Tragedy of Labour*, Basil Blackwell, Oxford, 1980

Hindess, Barry, *The Decline of Working Class Politics*, MacGibbon and Kee, London, 1971

Hodgson, Geoff, *Labour at the Crossroads*, Martin Robertson, Oxford, 1981

Hoggart, Simon, and Leigh, David, *Michael Foot: a Portrait*, Hodder and Stoughton, London, 1981

Hunter, Leslie, *The Road to Brighton Pier*, Arthur Barker, London, 1959

Jenkins, Mark, *Bevanism: Labour's High Tide*, Spokesman, Nottingham, 1979

Jenkins, Robert, *Tony Benn: A Political Biography*, Writers and Readers, London, 1980

Kogan, David, and Kogan, Maurice, *The Battle for the Labour Party*, 2nd edn, Kogan Page, London, 1983

Lee, Jennie, *My Life With Nye*, Jonathan Cape, London, 1980

McCormick, Paul, *Enemies of Democracy*, Temple Smith, London, 1979

Mitchell, Austin, *Four Years in the Death of the Labour Party*, Methuen, London, 1983

Nightingale, Martyn, *et al.*, *Merseyside in Crisis*, Merseyside Socialist Research Group, Birkenhead, 1980

Pelling, Henry, *A Short History of the Labour Party*, Macmillan, London, 1961

Pelling, Henry, *The British Communist Party*, Adam and Charles Black, London, 1975

Pimlott, Ben, *Labour and the Left in the 1930s*, Cambridge University Press, Cambridge, 1977

Shipley, Peter, *Revolutionaries in Modern Britain*, Bodley Head, London, 1976

Shipley, Peter, *The Militant Tendency*, Foreign Affairs Publishing Co., London, 1983

Spiers, John (ed.), *The Left in Britain: A Checklist and Guide*, The Harvester Press, Brighton, 1976

Taaffe, Peter, *What We Stand For*, Militant, London, 1981

BIBLIOGRAPHY

Tatchell, Peter, *The Battle for Bermondsey*, Heretic Books, London, 1983

Thayer, George, *The British Political Fringe*, Anthony Blond, London, 1965

Tomlinson, John, *Left, Right: The March of Political Extremism in Britain*, John Calder, London, 1981

Waller, P. J., *Democracy and Sectarianism: A Political and Social History of Liverpool 1868–1939*, Liverpool University Press, Liverpool, 1982

Weighell, Sidney, *On the Rails*, Orbis, London, 1983

Widgery, David, *The Left in Britain 1956–68*, Penguin, Harmondsworth, 1976

Williams, Philip, *Hugh Gaitskell: A Political Biography*, Jonathan Cape, London, 1979

Willis, Ted, *Whatever Happened to Tom Mix? The Story of One of My Lives*, Cassell, London, 1970

Woods, A., and Grant, T., *Lenin and Trotsky: What They Really Stood For*, Militant, London, 1969

Young, Alison, *The Reselection of MPs*, Heinemann Educational, London, 1983

Index

INDEX

North, 175–7, 179; and Labour's
1982 Conference, 180–2; press
relations, 187–9; expulsions from
Labour Party, 190–8, 211; and
the Bermondsey by-election, 194;
1983 election, 9–11, 144, 198,
202–3, 217–18; appeals against
expulsions, 201; isolation, 201–3;
and non-party political groups,
203–4; reselection of MPs, 206; at
Labour Conferences, 207; NEC's
powerlessness against, 210–12;
candidates for NEC, 213–14
Militant, 10, 41, 79, 97, 170; and the
RSL, 11n.; NEC expels Editorial
Board members, 15, 16;
forerunners, 43; first issues, 45–9;
and *Left*, 55; buys printing press,
59–60; and the CWI, 110–11;
expansion, 116; circulation, 116,
125; Fighting Fund, 116–17,
121–2; costs, 129; readers' rally,
189; Golding takes legal action
against, 189–90; ban on sales at
Labour Party meetings, 200, 205;
industrial news, 203
Militant (RCP), 37
Militant (USA), 32, 46
Militant International Review, 101,
108
Militant Irish Monthly, 110–12
Militant Labour League, 28, 32–4
Militant Miner, 108
Militant Teacher, 108
Mooney, Edward, 119
Morgan, Steve, 59
Morning Star, 117, 188
Morrison, Herbert, 23, 36
Mortimer, Jim, 99; and the
Proscribed List, 21–2, 26;
sponsors *The Week*, 48–9; and the
register, 179; attacks Militant,
181, 188, 189; and the right wing
takeover of the NEC, 184; lists
Militant workers, 185–6; Militant
expulsions, 190–3, 198, 204; 1983
election, 200
Mulhearn, Tony, 119, 144, 169,
186, 207, 215

NALGO, 136, 158, 168
NALGO Militant, 108
National Association for Freedom,
88
National Association of Labour
Student Organizations,
49
National Executive Committee
(NEC), 94, 99, 170; and the
suppression of *Socialist Outlook*,
15, 22; relations with Communist
Party, 18; Bevanite split, 23–5;
and Communist infiltration, 31–
2; and the LPYS review, 54–5;
LPYS representative, 59, 79;
Militant attempts to gain
membership of, 61, 213–14;
Underhill reports, 85–7, 163–5;
Organization Sub-Committee, 86,
175, 176, 188–9, 190–1, 192;
Bevan affair, 91–2; election
manifestos, 162, 165; inquiry into
Militant, 173–5, 177, 179, 181,
200; and Bradford North, 175–6;
swings to right, 182, 184–5;
Militant expulsions, 15, 16, 190–
8; 1983 election, 200; powerless to
stop Militant, 210–11
National Front, 72, 210–11
National Graphical Association
(NGA), 127
National Organization of Labour
Students (NOLS), 78–84, 126,
135, 174, 204
National Union of Journalists
(NUJ), 127, 157, 177
National Union of Labour
Organizers, 92
National Union of Mineworkers
(NUM), 168, 182
National Union of Railwaymen
(NUR), 168
National Union of Students (NUS),
83
nationalization, 63–5, 74
NATO, 73
Nava Sama Samaji Party (NSSP),
112
Nazism, 19, 29, 165